The Life and Times of
Cozy Eggleston
and His Jazz Band

Featuring His Wife, Marie Stone

Connie J. Eggleston MSW, CPM

PAGE PUBLISHING
Conneaut Lake, PA

First originally published by Page Publishing 2023

ISBN 979-8-88793-064-0 (pbk)
ISBN 979-8-88793-097-8 (digital)

Printed in the United States of America

In loving memory of my one and only son, Sababu Kalonji Omobowale Meeks.

Contents

Preface

Listening to my dad, CJ "Cozy" Eggleston, over the years, telling me about his life, inspired the writing of this book. I wanted to have a historical account of my parents' extraordinary and interesting lives to leave their legacy. Also, this account would give my current and future generations knowledge of their ancestors. In addition, it would give people insight into the lives of jazz musicians. My parents were artists who traveled to make a decent living. In addition, this book details the evolution of music in this country from its beginning to now. My siblings and I spent about five years without our parents. During that era, most artists traveled without their children. This was not unusual. However, most women didn't travel with their husbands and were able to care for their children at home. In this case, my mother was a member of her husband's band, playing the alto saxophone. So my grandmother, who was single at that time, accepted the responsibility of caring for us. We went to live with her in Cairo, Illinois. After five years under her care, there was an event that changed our lives. My grandmother could no longer take care of us because she had a serious stroke. So my parents had to care for us again. They stopped road travel and moved my siblings and me back to Chicago.

I have fond memories of living in Cairo and in Chicago. I describe those impressionable times in my life, especially my parents' role. One may wonder why I detailed these events. It's because I want people to know the importance of having guidance from both parents, especially a father figure. My dad was an exemplary role model to his and other neighborhood children. Later in life, during adulthood, I moved away on my own. I went to college, had a family and children, and obtained employment that sent me up to Oklahoma. I always remembered what my parents taught me, which carried me through rough times. While working, I would always use my vacation time to make visits to Chicago. I would not go to any other place because my parents were getting up in age. I wanted to spend as much time as I could with them. I was devastated when my mother, Frances Marie "Stone" Eggleston, passed in May 2002. I started visiting my dad as often as I could. I retired in August 2007 from a twenty-six-year career in the state government. This gave me the opportunity to spend more time with my dad.

People say that men remember history better than women. Talking to my dad over the years seems to validate this theory. So I realized I must get the story of his life which, of course, included my mom. During a visit to Chicago in September 2007, a month after my retirement, I recorded my dad. We had a delightful time. It was the best quality time spent with him and the most memorable too. This is for you, Pops and Mom, with much love.

Acknowledgments

I want to acknowledge those who gave support and information toward this project as follows: my daughter Dr. Feyisetan Lott (physician) and her husband, James (when I was in need, they gave me a place of respite in their home); Jeff Ash, a writer/journalist who researched and contributed many articles and pictures of my parents for me to use (he resides in Green Bay, Wisconsin, where my parents performed many times); and my sister Rosemarie Eggleston, a retired Chicago County sheriff (She found many pictures for our family tree and remembered things I couldn't).

Much appreciation for Beverly Melvin, a friend and confidant over the years.

I can't omit my precious pet, Copper. She's my road dog when I travel by car. She accompanies me on my daily walks so we both can stay fit and healthy. Everybody loves Copper.

I want to acknowledge my grandchildren—Jasmyn Marie, Falyn Bree, and Jalen Kennedy Lott. Their love and vibrancy, being so full of energy and life, inspire me to keep on pushing.

Also, my loving brothers James Eggleston and Cletus Ray who inspire me.

In addition, thanks to Eddie Jones for his unwavering support and input.

Finally, I thank almighty God. Without Him, I don't know where I'd be.

I give my sincere thanks to all.

In the Beginning

It was a scorching hot day in May 1920. The baseball stadium was packed to capacity with people. The pitcher struck out the batter with a hard and fast curveball. The pitcher stood on top of the mound, getting ready to throw his next pitch. The fans, eating their popcorn and hotdogs, were waiting for the next batter. The next batter was swinging his bat before stepping up to the home plate. Realistically, the crowd really came to see him. There had been a lot of chatter about him among baseball fans. It was Babe Ruth. The crowd cheered as he stepped up to the plate. The stadium became so quiet that one could hear a pin drop.

"Strike one!" the umpire yelled.

The pitcher shrugged his shoulders, rolling the ball around in his hand. Babe Ruth hovered over the plate ready for the pitch. The pitcher threw the ball in angst. *Crack!* was the sound of the bat hitting the ball. The fans followed the ball with their eyes, going, going, gone as the ball went into the stands. It was a home run! The crowd cheered as Babe Ruth ran around the bases. He'd hit his first home run. My grandmother Mattie gave birth to my father nine days later. It could be the reason my dad was so interested in baseball. Just a thought.

My father, CJ "Cozy" Eggleston, was born on May 10, 1920. In the month of my dad's birth, on May 1, 1920, Babe Ruth (of the New York Yankees) hit his first Major League Baseball home run. On September 24 of that same year, Babe Ruth hit his fiftieth home run. He was quite a slugger. He passed away in August 1948—a couple of months before my birth in October. Babe Ruth was the "talk of the nation" during the era of my father's early life. He would always tell us stories about baseball and Babe Ruth, who was famous when he was born. In addition, an important event during the time of my father's birth was the organization of the first Black baseball league, called the National Negro Baseball League.

Baseball truly influenced him. He was a fan of Major League Baseball and loved watching it. In our household, as in many in the US during my early childhood, there was only one TV set per family. My dad would take over the TV whenever the channel aired a baseball game. My siblings and I would turn to other channels to keep my father from knowing about a baseball game airing. He would find out, so we had to watch too.

My dad loved baseball so much that he would come to our grammar school and take us out of class to attend the White Sox baseball games. That became a great tradition. We lived close to the Chicago White Sox baseball stadium, called Comiskey Park at that time. It was within walking distance. I loved seeing my tall-in-stature dad standing up front in class. He was talking to my teacher to get permission to take me out of class to attend the baseball game. The teacher appeared happy to see a father figure represented in a family. The teacher always obliged with permission to my dad's request. During those times, there weren't many father figures in the households in my neighborhood. My dad served the role of a father figure to many neighborhood children. Although I was elated to see my dad, knowing he was there to take us out of school to attend a game, I wasn't interested in the game. I was just happy to get out of school. Of course, I did have fun, just being out of school and participating as a spectator. My dad purchased popcorn, candy, and pop to enjoy. That was the best part. I loved the Babe Ruth candy bar. Woodrow Wilson was still president when my dad was born; however, he lost his presidency to Warren D. Hardy on March 4, 1921. Later in life, my father became interested in music. He told me he started learning how to play the saxophone while in the army.

On the day my mother was born, March 6, 1918, a US naval boat called the *Cyclops* disappeared in the Bermuda Triangle. My mother had always thought she was born on March 6, 1918. Much later in life, she saw on her official birth certificate a birthday date of March 7, 1918. It was only one day off, so she continued to celebrate her birthday on March 6. In 1918, my mother's birth year, there was a horrible flu epidemic killing many US citizens, somewhat like COVID-19 now. My parents were newborns and were not part of the group with a high death rate, so they survived. The very young had a very low fatality rate for the flu. Both parents were very young during the time period between August 1929 through March 1933—the Great Depression.

Later in life, my mother's interest in learning how to play musical instruments began when she was in high school. She developed a love for music. She told me she took music classes and learned how to play the clarinet and the flute. As previously mentioned, my father became interested in playing an instrument when he entered the army. They both attended the Chicago Conservatory of Music to further pursue a knowledge of music. My parents made it through those trying times of events that occurred after they were born. Little did they know how much music would impact their lives.

2

The Influence of Music in America

As one can see, my parents were born during times of much hardship. There were a lot of tragic and other important events happening during and after the time of my parents' births. However, there was a specific genre that intertwined people for the good of all mankind. The genre was music, and it was a very significant era of historical importance. Music had a major impact on the lives of my parents and our family as well. It shaped the very essence and dynamics of our family throughout the years.

Music is an integral part of American culture. Dictionary.com defines *music* as "an art of sound in time that expresses ideas and emotions in significant forms through the elements of rhythm, melody, harmony, and color." Native Americans were the original inhabitants of America. One cannot talk about the beginning of music without including them. Native American folk music was the main form of music centering around religion. When Europeans came to America, "Native American folk music blended with European folk music in the 1500s once they started invading" (PianoTV 2018). Appalachian folk music or hillbilly music mixes Black and White American,

Irish, and Scottish styles. Considered early types of country music are honky-tonk and bluegrass.

Africans torn away from their country to toil on American soil brought their version of folk music. Their work songs were prevalent during that time. Many songs had hidden messages that gave instructions on escaping to the north in pursuit of freedom. In addition, they had to do something to ease the pain of the whippings they were given. It helped their psyche, lessening the hardship of the work they endured in the hot fields. Spiritual music became very popular among African Americans in the 1700s in the south. Also in the 1700s, American pop music became popular, with singers like William Billings, along with ballads and patriotic songs. In essence, the roots of pop music came from blues and jazz.

3

The Evolution of Jazz

It's for certain that jazz started in the United States of America beginning in the late 1800s. Blues emanated from the South. It "evolved from hymns, work songs, and field hollers…is the foundation of jazz…the prime source of rhythm and blues, rock 'n' roll, and country music" ("Culture & Change: Black History in America," Scholastic Teacher's Activity Guide).

African Americans used blues to help them get through societal injustices and adversity. Many African American blues artists sang about broken hearts from love or romantic relationships and hardships. Some feel that jazz stemmed from blues, and others don't. They feel jazz has its own developmental genre and beginning. During my adult years, I preferred jazz over blues. I felt that Blacks didn't need music to make us sad and that jazz was more powerful. I felt that blues lyrics sang about gloom and doom such as "My Baby Done Left Me." Why listen to or promote blues songs when Blacks already face a lot of sadness and adversity? Move on and be happy.

When people would ask me if my parents were blues musicians, I responded with an emphatic no. My parents, especially my father, felt the same way. He would always tell people he didn't play the blues and that his form of music was jazz. When I heard Wynton Marselis explain it in the article cited, he gave me a different outlook on the sadness with blues. He used a music segment of an instrumental played by John Coltrane, then asked listeners to snap their fingers on the second and fourth beats. He indicated that adding the sound of the rhythm from the beat brought forth a happier feeling. I agreed, which gave me a better understanding of blues. Jazz had its beginnings in the Black community of New Orleans, Louisiana. Jazz music emerged during the late nineteenth to early twentieth century, with its roots in ragtime and blues. "Jazz music, which had originated in New Orleans in the early 1900s, began to spread throughout the country by the late teens… From its beginnings until the 50's jazz was a utilitarian music intended mostly for dancing" (Jazz Standards.com/history/index.htm).

4

Jazz and the Harlem Renaissance

The Harlem Renaissance was at the forefront of the evolution of music in America from the 1910s through the mid-1930s. The Harlem Renaissance gave way to new energy in African American culture. It brought to life its music, dance, theater, and fashion trends. During the era of the Harlem Renaissance, African American scholars emerged in areas of literature and politics. Main figures of the literary Harlem Renaissance were Jean Toomer, Jessie Fauset, Claude McKay, James Weldon Johnson, Zora Neale Hurston, and Langston Hughes. The geographic location of Harlem Renaissance activities occurred in Harlem, Manhattan, in New York City during the 1920s and the 1930s.

Because of migration and other extenuating circumstances, Harlem became one of the largest Black communities in the country. Many African Americans left the south and moved to Harlem because sharecropping jobs were shrinking because of natural disasters in 1915 and 1916. "By 1920, some 300,000 African Americans from the South had moved north, and Harlem was one of the most popular destinations for these families" (History.com editors 2009). The Harlem Renaissance produced a major form of music called jazz. Jazz was the dominant musical force in that era.

In the 1920s, jazz artists such as trumpet player Louis Armstrong became a member of Fletcher Henderson's band. When Armstrong became a member, the trumpet player changed the sound of Henderson's band. "Another New Orleans native, Sydney Betchet, player of the soprano saxophone, caused a similar change in the orchestra of Duke Ellington" (Jazz Standards.com). Despite changes in the sounds played by saxophonists in that era, with these artists including Coleman Hawkins, tenor saxophonists would remain dominant. This trend was popular until saxophonist Lester Young emerged during the '30s. Lester Young played the tenor saxophone, as did my father. While I was recording him telling his life story, he referred to Lester Young by his nickname Prez. They called Lester Young "Prez" because he was considered the "president of jazz" throughout the country. Actually, singer Billie Holiday gave Lester Young his nickname. "Prez's sound marked the beginning of modern jazz." My father told me during our conversation that Lester Young was his idol. He tried to mimic Young's sound when he played his tenor saxophone. He stated, "Everyone was trying to sound like the Prez." It was only later that my father decided to develop his own sound and style of play.

Not only was jazz popular among Black Harlem residents, but Whites outside of the area enjoyed it too. Some famous musicians performing in Harlem included Louis Armstrong, Duke Ellington, Cab Calloway, and Fats

Waller. They became popular celebrities and prominent Black figures during the time of the Harlem Renaissance. These Black musicians had to have a place to perform. One such place was the Savoy, an integrated club of Blacks and Whites, which opened in 1927 in Harlem. It was a very popular club that offered jazz music and a huge dance floor for its patrons. However, not all Whites wanted to mix with Blacks to experience their culture. So came the founding of the Cotton Club, where many Black musicians performed to White-only audiences.

5

Jazz and All of That Jazz

No matter the scene, during the period of the Harlem Renaissance, music was the root of it all, with the jazz age at the forefront. The jazz age, 1920–1929, brought about more interest in African American culture. It occurred simultaneously with the Harlem Renaissance. During the jazz age, there were changing roles for women and more jobs for them. The women called themselves flappers. These flappers changed their behavior from what society thought was proper for them. They wore shorter skirts and their hair in a short bob style. They were somewhat rebellious, refusing to fit the norm of the society of how they should act. Their behavior engulfed actions of more sexual freedom. Also, during that time, women were very fond of jazz.

Jazz and the Harlem Renaissance made it all possible. The Roaring Twenties, 1920–1929, was a part of this jazz age. Economic growth among many Americans was at its height. More citizens than ever in American history lived in cities instead of on farms. Purchasing television sets, radios, automobiles, electric refrigerators, and other luxuries became a national phenomenon. The prohibition of alcohol heightened as laws were passed to curb consumption.

Dances popular during that time were the black bottom, the cakewalk, the flea hop, and the Charleston. My mother taught my siblings and me how to do the Charleston. She put both palms of her hands on both knees and moved them inward and outward. You switch out hands on each one with every move, giving the illusion of a wave of ripple. If done correctly, it looks like a continuous movement wave or ripple. My siblings and I loved to dance, and my parents knew it. We were so good that every time they had company over, they would call us to dance for them. Dancing carried over into my college days too.

Jazz set the standard for many musicians. With the evolution of the radio, many more Americans were able to listen to jazz. They didn't have to buy clothes to wear or pay costs to go to a club to hear jazz. They could stay in the confines of their homes. All they had to do was just turn on their radios. In the 1920s, the introduction of sound became a part of motion picture production. Instead of silent movies, constituents could hear jazz music while watching movies. Another contributing factor in disseminating music for musicians during the '20s was the phonograph. This was an evolving trend for the music industry which eliminated piano rolls and sheet music. Independent record companies like Gennett and Paramount started recording smaller jazz performers from Chicago on their labels. Records was another venue used to disseminate music to the general public. States records recorded my father's songs on its label in 1954. I was only six years old at the time. To hear one of his songs called "Cozy's Boogie" on the States label, go to https://youtu.be/Ya6cgo6g3es.

Correction: In this video, they state my father's name is Cyril "Cozy" Eggleston. His name is CJ "Cozy" Eggleston.

45worlds

Visit

78 RPM - Cozy Eggleston - Cozy's Boogie / Big Heavy - States - USA ...

45worlds

Visit

78 RPM - Cozy Eggleston - Cozy's Boogie / Big Heavy - States - USA...

Different jazz styles

Jazz emerged in various forms. As previously mentioned, the early jazz style of music was ragtime originating in New Orleans. Band members played the clarinet, trombone, and wind instruments played on upbeats called syncopations. An example of a song with syncopation is George Gershwin's "Summertime," used in the musical *Porgy and Bess* in 1935.

Jazz artists created various sounds. A jazz pianist named Fletcher Henderson, out of New York, had a twelve-piece band called a dance orchestra. Some past music enthusiasts didn't consider ragtime as jazz. Henderson's style of ragtime music was influenced by jazz. Ragtime is "a rhythm characterized by strong syncopation in the melody with a regularly accented accompaniment in stride-piano style" (*Merriam-Webster*). More simply put, according to the Learners Dictionary, it is "a type of lively music that is often played on the piano and that was very popular in the US in the early part of the 20th century." Some popular ragtime songs are "The Entertainer" and "Maple Leaf" by Scott Joplin, often called the king of ragtime.

Swing jazz. During the 1930s—the time of the Great Depression and the swing era—jazz music flourished via jazz artist Benny Goodman. Benny Goodman, nicknamed "King of Swing," performed at the very first ever jazz concert in Carnegie Hall. This sparked a significant rise in other artists to perform jazz with solos and jazz arrangements. "Swing, also called 'Big Band,' is characterized by a forward propulsion imparted to each note by players" (Wharton Center 2015). Swing bands usually had at least ten members and favored dancers. Swing music became a medium for dancers because of its sounds and beats. Those who danced to the music did the Lindy Hop, jitterbug, boogie-woogie, East and West Coast Swings, and the Lindy Charleston, just to name a few. To hear an example of swing in Count Basie's song "One O'clock Jump," visit https://youtu.be/e4LEL3OREKE.

Bebop jazz. Bebop referred to itself as an art form, not as commercial dance music like swing. Evolving in the mid-1940s, Bebop is a more complicated music form than swing. Its music had more of a harmonic and a melodic sound.

I recall writing a paper while in college on the historical development of different music genres in America. Of course, I went straight to the source of someone who had much knowledge on the subject. That person was my father. I interviewed my father and vividly remember him voicing the sounds and rhythm of bebop. He called it hot jazz and remembered Louis Armstrong and his Hot Five name. My father really got into it. His whole mood would change, with his face lighting up anytime he talked about music in any form. As he described bebop, the sounds were coming from his mouth; it was as if he was actually playing it on his tenor saxophone. He was using scat singing. "Scat singing along with soloist improvisation is commonly used to accompany the rhythm of Bebop tunes" (Wharton Center 2015).

The singer Ella Fitzgerald sang songs doing scat. Famous bebop songs from that time include "A Night in Tunisia" by Charlie Parker and "Salt Peanuts" by Dizzy Gillespie. These two were the top jazz artists in that era and codified as the inventors of bebop. Musician-composer Charlie "Bird" Parker played jazz bebop on the alto and tenor saxophone from 1937 to 1955. Dizzy Gillespie, called the Ambassador of Jazz, played the trumpet. People gave him this title because he organized a band and played in Africa, Asia, and the Middle East as part of a State Department tour. He was known for his balloon-like cheeks, which expanded as he blew his trumpet. Gillespie was seventy-five years of age when he passed on January 6,

1993. My dad told me Louis Armstrong named his trumpet Satchmo and engraved that name on his horn. To hear a sample of bebop played by Dizzy Gillespie, go to https://youtu.be/09BB1pci8_o.

Hard-bop jazz. Hard-bop music surfaced between 1955 and 1956, with influences from blues, soul, and gospel. "*New York Herald Tribune* music critic John Mehegan is credited with coming up with the term *hard bop* which was developed as an East Coast alternative to the cool jazz style which was coming out of California" (Matt Fripp 2021). Hard bop is a form of bebop music; however, hard bop focuses on the drum. The musician Art Blakey's hard bop contributed to highlighting solos for the drum in music. Even James Brown hollered out in one of his songs, "Give the drummer some." Hard bop has not really died out over the years. Some jazz artists such as Herbie Hancock, Thelonious Monk, and Miles Davis used it in their music. Popular hard-bop songs include "Somethin' Else" by Cannonball Adderly, "Blue Train" by John Coltrane, "Relaxin'" by Miles Davis, and "Saxophone Colossus" by Sonny Rollins. To hear an example of hard-bop music played by John Coltrane, visit https://youtu.be/wy6115CsV_Y.

Post-bop / nonfree jazz. Post-bop jazz was popular from 1958 to 1973 with a style that is hard to identify. Basically, it is a modern reexamination and restructuring of the elements of bop music. Instruments used in post-bop jazz include the saxophone, trumpet, drums, clarinet, piano, trombone, and double bass. The song "A Love Supreme" by saxophonist John Coltrane in 1964 is an example of post-bop jazz. The band leader and trumpet player Miles Davis were at the forefront of the post-bop sound. Pianist Herbie Hancock was another great leader in post-bop jazz and a member of the Miles Davis Quintet. He was instrumental in creating the aspect of the jazz rhythm section in music while playing in the quintet. To hear an example of post-bop jazz played by Miles Davis in the song "The Sorcerer," visit https://youtu.be/hGyCGvu5BMc.

Cool jazz. Cool jazz emerged in the 1940s after World War II through around 1964. It utilizes more relaxed tempos with a lighter tone unlike the more complex and fast bebop style of music. Its sound utilizes more formal arrangements as found in classical music. "Cool jazz…was slow, soft, light lyrical, low pitched, low energy and sparse. There were a number of early jazz musicians who inspired the 'Cool' way of playing, including: Bix Beiderbecke, Frankie Trumbauer, and especially, Lester Young—who was really the forefather of Cool Jazz" (http://www.thejazzpianosite. com). Examples of cool jazz songs are "So What" by Miles Davis, "Girl from Ipanema" by Stan Getz, "Take Five" by the Dave Brubeck Quartet, and "My Favorite Things" by John Coltrane. To hear Stan Getz play cool jazz with the song "The Girl from Ipanema," visit https://youtu.be/ c5QfXjsoNe4.

Free jazz. The free, or avant-garde, jazz style of music does not stem from bebop. It surfaced between 1950 and 1980. Free-jazz musicians are soloists who do not play in an ensemble band with other musicians. In free-jazz music, there is no musical arrangement or cord progression. When one hears more than two notes at once, it's considered a chord. Musicians who play free jazz are not bound by any fixed structure and can play whatever they wish. To hear an example of free jazz played by Ornette Coleman, go to https://youtu.be/8bRTFr0ytA8. The Pharoah Sanders album Karma is another example of free-jazz music.

Fusion jazz. Fusion, or electric jazz, is a style of music that mixes funk, soul, and rock into one sound. It gained popularity from 1964 through 1984. Artists/groups considered "fusioneers" are Chick Corea, the Crusaders, Herbie Hancock, Freddie Hubbard, John McLaughlin, Grover Washington Jr., and Weather Report. To hear an example of fusion jazz played by Freddie Hubbard in his song "Straight Life," visit https://youtu.be/a4xwNHUyz1Q.

6

The Eggleston Family Tree

Over the years, I listened to my father talk about his life. He was very descriptive and really enjoyed it. I wanted to capture his life stories in writing. I decided the way to do this was with a book. When I retired from the Oklahoma state government in 2007, I traveled to my birthplace, Chicago, to visit my father to get started on the book. The best way to get the story was to record it. So I purchased some blank tapes and used my daddy's recorder. My dad loved champagne. So I purchased some for him. We toasted with the beautiful glasses he and Mom had collected over the years and began the recording. Dad would always talk about his family tree, so that was where we started.

He started talking about his family tree and a man named James "Jim" Eggleston. I said, "So your history comes from Jim Eggleston?"

He said, "Yes, Grandpa. He was a White man who married my grandmother's sister out of slavery. The first sister's mother got Jim to marry her daughter out of slavery. After she died, he married my grandmother. Her name was Lola. She was the younger sister of the first lady he married. So Jim married two sisters. I don't remember my grandmother's sister's name. The first sister had two children, Uncle Oliver and Aunt Addie Eggleston. My grandmother Lola had seven kids, I think. There was Uncle Clark, Uncle Sol, Uncle Doney, LC, who was my father, Aunt Darlissy, Aunt Julie, and Aunt Jenny. There were seven children."

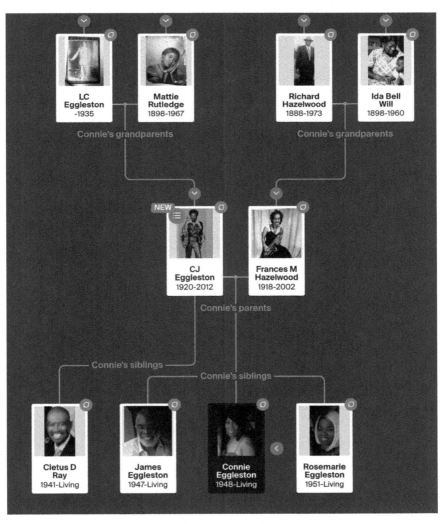

Eggleston Family Tree

So I tried to recap the family tree. Jim Eggleston married Lola, the second sister. She had seven children, and Dad's father (LC) was one of the children. LC married my dad's mother, Mattie Beatrice Johnson. They conceived my dad, CJ, who is the only child from that marriage. Cozy was born on May 12, 1920, to LC and Mattie B. Eggleston.

I asked," How do you remember your dad?"

As a child, he said, he would make runs with his father to bootleg alcohol during days of prohibition.

I asked, "When did your dad pass?"

He replied, "In 1935." His father, LC, passed away when my dad, CJ "Cozy," was fifteen years old. His death left his mother, Mattie, a single mom to raise her son. So my father was an only child whose mother reared him as a single mom since his father passed. They were very close.

Rearing a Son as a Single Parent

Mattie was a God-fearing, staunch, robustly built matriarchal figure. CJ said his mother reared him with an iron hand, with him being all boy. Believe me, my dad told me he was definitely all boy. Whenever he told me stories over the phone about his childhood, he could make me visualize everything. Once, he told me how he did something that really upset his mother. He didn't tell me what it was, but she tied him to the bedpost to give him a whipping. Back in those days, whippings were a part of parental discipline techniques. Nowadays, I guess it would be called child abuse.

Mattie was a spiritually grounded mother. She instilled that good old-time religion into her son. Dad recollected his days of going to church. His mother hardly ever missed a Sunday. He would wake up to the smell of his mother's Sunday cooking. There were after-church gatherings. Mattie would cook and take her food to church along with other members of the congregation. They would attend Sunday school in the morning, a regular church service later in the morning, and the feast afterward. They'd return home late at night.

During baptism, Mattie took CJ to church down by the river. It was the day that Mattie explained to her son the meaning of getting the Holy Spirit. His mother told him that he must get the Holy Spirit to be saved. CJ lined up along the bank of the river with others to get the Holy Spirit. He noticed that when others were being baptized, they would cry and gyrate. However, when it was CJ's turn, he could neither gyrate nor cry. Well, on the way home, Mattie told CJ that he was going to get severely punished if he did not get the Holy Spirit. When it came to the next baptism, CJ was still not "getting the Holy Spirit." Remembering what his mother had told him about a punishment, CJ placed fake tears in his eyes with his saliva and began a bogus gyration. She fell for it too. He made his mother proud and avoided punishment at the same time. My dad didn't want me to mention this here, but I did. He can't do anything about it now.

Later, Mattie and CJ moved to Chicago in 1933. I asked Dad, "What made you come to Chicago?"

He replied, "I don't know." Dad said he was about thirteen years of age at that time. He continued, "We moved back to Cairo, Illinois, around 1934."

I asked, "Did you stay in Chicago?"

He raised his voice a little bit and said, "No, I didn't stay here. I went back home too. I left home again in 1937 to come back to Chicago."

I asked, "What made you come back? Did you get sick of Cairo?"

He replied, "No, I just wanted to come back to get a job."

Later, his mother, Mattie, married Mr. George Rutledge.

24

8

Cozy's Beginnings
Playing the Saxophone

I asked my dad why he wanted to play the tenor sax.

He said, "I wanted to play music and back in 1937–1938." Cozy reminisced, saying, "I went back home to Cairo in 1939 for Christmas. I stayed down there for about a year. I came back to Chicago. I remember when Lester Young came to Chicago with Count Basie's band. They were playing at the Grand Terrace. My friends and I, who were around 17–18 years of age, had no music to listen to except for Count Basie's. Lester Young played the tenor saxophone in Basie's band. I heard Lester Young." That's when Dad took a keen interest in Lester. He listened to Lester's music. He said, "I could whistle all of Lester's solos, note for note, that were on Basie's records."

He then told me, "My friend Lester Young became my inspiration to play the tenor saxophone. I decided to buy me a horn. I bought me a horn and, uh, I bought one out of the pawnshop. I bought my first horn in 1940. I wanted to play music. My cousin went with me to buy the horn. He was blind and was an alto saxophonist. So I saw this horn and told the man I wanted that one. I thought I was buying a tenor saxophone, but I was buying a C melody. It has the same pitch as a piano. My cousin was blind, and he could not tell me the difference between the horns. I kept it anyway. So when I got home, I played the scale up, but I could not play it down." Dad learned how to play his sax on his own at age twenty.

I said to my dad, "You had never played a sax before. Never touched a saxophone?"

He said, "I played Tuxedo Junction. I am not kidding you." He started singing the melody and said, "I played Erskine Hawkins's song. I played this the same day I purchased the horn."

I told him it was amazing how he could play music without having had formal lessons. He said that later, he had gone to the CC camp in Skokie, Illinois. He stopped playing his horn.

9

Learning How to Play the Saxophone

He went on to say, "I came back to Chicago in 1942. They shipped us out, uh, back in the day. The war was going on. You'd go up to the Social Security board, and they'd ship a bunch out to Salt Lake City, Utah. They shipped us out there to build a naval base. The Social Security Board was at Forty-Seventh and King Drive. It was South Park then. We went out there, and I stayed out there at the naval base until Christmas." When Dad came back to Chicago, he had a job at the Swift meat and packing company. Cozy also held a job at a Chicago stockyard.

He said, "I came back home and went into the army." While working at Swift, the army drafted him in 1943. He stated, "Everybody wanted to play a saxophone after they heard Lester Young. He was a wonderful cat. He had a style of his own. All of the saxophone players copied him."

I asked, "You didn't copy him, did you? You had your own style?"

He continued, "No, I copied him. However, I went away from him. After I started playing, I went away from him and started playing some of his things, but I still got my own style."

I asked, "How did you learn how to play? Because it's hard. I remember how difficult it was when you tried to teach me on Mom's horn."

He said, "I bought me another horn in January 1944." It wasn't until he joined the army that he began practicing on his horn again. Cozy said, "I bought me a tenor when I went into the army in 1944 in Cheyenne, Wyoming, at Fort Warren. I used to go to the band room during the day. We worked nights until twelve o'clock when all of the soldiers had to be out of town. I was a military policeman. I used to go to the band room every day. We worked nights down in Cheyenne, Wyoming. A boy from Chicago I knew was in the band they had in the army. I started taking lessons. They were teaching me. All the old guys were teaching me."

I asked, "How long did it take you to learn how to play it?"

He said, "It didn't take me long. I was playing when I came out of the army." He served in the army until 1945.

I commented, "So from 1920 to 1945, you were twenty-five years old. Did you learn how to read music?"

Dad continued his recollection and said, "When I got ready to come out of the army, I sent my horn to Elkhart, Indiana, to let them put gold lacquer on it. It had silver lacquer on it. I had it repaired. When I came back home, they shipped me my horn. I was playing then. When I got out of the army, I started taking lessons in downtown Chicago."

I asked," Did you take other lessons?"

He said, "I took lessons at the Midwestern Conservatory of Music College."

I asked, "How long did you go to college?"

He said." I went for about three years."

I asked, "Do you still try to sound like Lester Young?"

He said, "Yeah, I'm still playing his thing. We became friends. He came to my house. When he'd come to Chicago, we'd go over to the Beehive to see him. Marie had a blond streak in her hair."

I asked him the year when that occurred, and he told me it was in the fifties.

He continued, "I knew Lester Young when I was in the army. He'd come to Cheyenne, Wyoming, to play with the All Stars. They had a USO band. He would also come to Chicago to play at the Grand Terrace with Count Basie. We all liked the way Prez sounded."

I asked, "Did Lester Young play the tenor sax?"

Dad responded, "Yeah, he had a tenor sax. He was the greatest tenor saxophone player that's been out here. There was Coleman Hawkins and all of the guys, but we went with Prez. All the tenor saxophone players all over the United States went with Prez. They continued to copy his style."

I asked Dad, "How did Lester Young get the name Prez?"

Dad said, "We called him Prez because he was the president of the saxophone. He was with the Count Basie Band. Gene Ammons, Dexter Gordon…all of those guys played tenor sax and wanted to sound like Prez."

Swift continued to pay Dad while he was in the army. They had his job waiting for him when he got out. Cozy was an only child who had great ambitions. He began as a self-taught saxophone player. While working at Swift, he continued to practice diligently on his horn. As CJ "Cozy" Eggleston began to get better at playing his sax, he felt he could make it on his own as a musician and resigned from the packing company. I asked him what else he did after he got out of the army.

He said, "I was playing while at the conservatory. I was playing at the Hurricane here in Chicago on Fifty-Fifth Street. I went and joined the musicians' union when I got out of the army. It was called Local 208. It was an all-Black union." Union musicians had to be paid based on an established scale. So their pay was better than non-union musicians. Of course, there are union dues. The American Federation of Musicians was formed in 1896. Chicago's Local 10 came into existence in 1901. Black musicians residing in Chicago tried to join Local 10 but weren't accepted due to their race. So Chicago's Black musicians formed Local 208, under the Chicago Federation of Musicians, in 1902.

As a little girl in Chicago, my siblings and I would leave school and walk to the Local 208 musicians' union, where our parents rehearsed. We knew all the administrators. My parents would always take us to the office to say hello to everyone, especially the union's president Mr. Harry Gray and his secretary. They would always say how much we had grown. There was a big black Doberman pincher dog there too behind an iron gate. I guess he must have been the guard dog. I don't remember the dog's name, but I do know one thing: he was a scary dog. He growled like crazy when we tried to approach the gate. We were certainly afraid of him.

There was a piano near the entryway of the building of Local 208. Once, my brother was sitting there, playing on the piano as if he was Beethoven. He was really going after it, improvising and moving his fingers across that keyboard like a professional musician. Later, a man who was a member of Local 208 approached my father. He told him my brother could really play that piano and that he had a nice sound. We were all cracking up because my brother was just improvising. Not a piano lesson my brother ever had. My dad just told the man thanks and never told him anything different. My siblings and I did have a good ear for music, more than likely from our genetic makeup, with both parents as musicians and all.

My siblings and I had so much fun, watching our parents and their band rehearse. There was a large room with a bandstand for Local 208 musicians to use to rehearse. We remembered all their songs. We knew the music so well that on many occasions when our parents couldn't remember the songs, they would ask us. We remembered every beat and rhythm. We'd hum or sing it out. We were their little assistants. "Racial segregation continued in the American Federation of Musicians for fifty-one years" (Julie Ayer 2005, as cited in Eastman School of Music, University of Rochester 2007).

During the height of the civil rights movement in the '60s, with integration and all, talk began about merging

Black and White musicians' unions. I vividly remember those times. There were some musicians who were for integrating unions, and some were not. My dad was adamant about not merging. He felt that they would lose their assets and their autonomy. He felt they would be swallowed up by Local 10, who had 11,000 members, with Local 208 having only 1,300 members. Also, there were others who felt that a merger shouldn't be forced either.

Well, those supporting the merger won. The Chicago Federation of Musicians Unions Local 208 and Local 10 officially merged on January 11, 1966. It was the beginning of Local 10-208. I found a list online of past presidents of Local 208 as follows:

Screenshot taken from the Chicago Federation of Musicians website.

LOCAL 208

1902-1904, Alexander Armand
1905-1907, J, B, Tucker
1908-1915, J, A, Smith
1916-1919, George A. Swann
1920-1921, Hugh Swift
1922-1923, George Smith
1924-1927, Dr, Robert Giles
1928-1929, Vernon Bigs
1930-1931, George Smith
1932-1938, Art Steward
1939-1965, Harry Gray

LOCALS 10 AND 208 MERGED ON JANUARY 11, 1966

Mr. Harry Gray was the president, as I remember going there, from the mid-'50s up to the time of the merger. He was the last president of Local 208. Mr. Gray held the office from 1939 to 1965. He held that office for thirty years—the longest-reigning Local 208 president of all others. Then came the merger of Local 10-208 in 1966.

10

Cozy's Career with
Lil Green's Band (1945–1946)

Lil Green

Cozy landed a job with Lil Green's band. Lillian "Lil" Green was a blues singer and songwriter who was born on December 22, 1919, in Mississippi and passed away on April 14, 1954, in Chicago, Illinois. As a teen, she sang gospel in the church. In addition to singing at church, she performed in juke joints in Mississippi. Later in her career, she moved to Chicago and began recording her songs (Wikipedia).

I asked Dad about his travels with Lil Green's band. He explained to me how he got into Lil Green's band.

He said, "Lil Green was singing with the Noel Cicero Band."

I asked, "Was he White?"

Dad said, "No, he was Black. There were no Blacks working with any White groups then except for Billie Holiday, who went with Artie Shaw's band."

I could barely make out the name from my dad's recording. It sounded like he was saying Arnie or Ollie Shaw, so I googled both names. The name Artie Shaw came up, indicating he was a band leader who was White. I asked Google if Billie Holiday ever sang in Artie Shaw's band and found this: "Billie Holiday by 1939 was a known singer in the New York jazz scene who had done brief stints as a big band vocalist with Count Basie and Artie Shaw in 1938. With Shaw's band, she became one of the first black women to work with a white orchestra" (The Pop History Dig 2011).

Dad continued, "So because of Lil Green's hit called 'Romance in the Dark,' everybody was playing it. Lil Green cut out and got her own band." Dad started singing, "Romance in the dark, just you and I."

I asked, "Was she older than you?"

He said, "Yes, she was in her thirties. She was a nice-looking woman. So Lil Green got real famous. Joe Glaser was one of the most famous booking agents in the

United States. He told her to get her a band. Lil Green had come to Chicago to get some musicians for her band."

Again, my father was correct in his recount of people's names and what they did, relating to jazz music. I googled the name *Joe Glaser*. He was a talent manager for jazz musicians and performing artists including Louis Armstrong and Billie Holiday. My dad wasn't just rambling. He had an excellent recall and knew what he was talking about with no hesitation.

Continuing by dad's story about Lil Green, he said, "So she got a seventeen-piece band together, and the tenor player's name was Johnny Sparrow. Johnny Sparrow, uh, who was with Lil Green and Noel Cicero? He came in here to take over the tenor section. Al King was in charge of the trombone section. Howard Chandler was in charge of the trumpet section." Dad continued, saying, "So while playing around here in Chicago at the 308 Club at the Ritz Hotel, Johnny Sparrow used to come down to the club and jam with me with my band because he liked my group."

I was in awe of all the names of the people he mentioned in his recount. Since my father is no longer here for me to go into details about his recount of names, places, and events, I completed a search and found information on a vast majority of his recount. He truly knew what he was talking about and remembered all the names of the people he came across in his career. Of course, I looked up Arvel Shaw too, who was born on September 15, 1923, in St. Louis, Missouri. The instrument he played was a double bass. He started out in high school, playing a tuba. However, while playing with Louis Armstrong, from 1942 to 1945, he switched to the double bass. Shaw passed on December 5, 2002 (Wikipedia).

Cozy went on to say that one day, the sax recruiter Johnny Sparrow said, "Cozy, why don't you come on out on the road with us?"

My dad said, "Man, I have never been out on the road with no band. I don't think I can make it. He kept asking me. He never gave up pursuing me. So I decided to go with them."

Arvell Shaw

Real Name:	Arvell Shaw
Profile:	American jazz double-bassist, best known for his work with Louis Armstrong.
	b. September 15, 1923 - St. Louis, Missouri.
	d. December 5, 2002 - Roosevelt, New York.

"The band traveled throughout the United States and overseas," he reminisced. "We traveled all over the United States, doing one-nighters."

The Lil Green band traveled all over the United States. I asked Dad how they traveled and if they were traveling by car.

Dad indicated that Lil Green's seventeen-piece band was prominent and had the luxury of traveling by Greyhound bus. Dad was calling out each city as if he was actually on the bus, traveling with the band. He stated, "Our first job was in Ashton, North Carolina. That was the first time we went out. Then we went all the way to Miami, Florida. We worked all over Miami. We worked in this town across this long bridge. I can't think of the name of that town now." He was rattling off the names of those cities like he was singing a song. "The band traveled to Delaware, Virginia, Alabama, New Orleans, Baton Rouge, and Phoenix." They also traveled on Route 66 to San Bernardino and to other cities along the West Coast. He continued, "We went from New Orleans all the way west to California. We went to sleep on the bus while traveling. We went up to San Francisco, Salt Lake City, and Denver, Colorado. We came back to play at the Army Hall in Chicago. Then we went to New York to play at the Apollo Theater. We played at the Cotton Club in New York. Cab Calloway played at the Cotton Club. They changed the name to the Sudan Club.

"I met Duke Ellington in Detroit. They closed at the Paradise Theater. Lil Green opened there the next day. Duke stayed over. I met him." Dad vividly remembered the conversation and said, "After we performed, I walked up to him and said, 'How are you doing, Mr. Ellington?' He said, 'Fine'. I told him this was my first time being on the road. Duke responded, Oh, it is. I could hear your horn playing over all the rest of them.'"

I said, "Dad, he told you that?"

Dad responded, "Then Duke said, 'But what I want you to do is get your own tone.' That was in 1945. By the way, the piano player who worked with us in Lil's band was Sonny Blount, birth name Herman Poole Blount. He later changed his name to Sun Ra. I went to see Sun Ra when he was playing at that club across from the Cubs' park, home of Chicago's baseball team. He was so happy to see me that he started shedding tears."

I asked, "Is he still living?"

Dad replied, "No, he died."

"Herman Poole Blount, better known as *Sun Ra,* rightfully gets credit for inventing *Afrofuturism,* the ingenious blend of sci-fi, Egyptology, occultism, and indigenous African spirituality" (Jones 2018). To hear Sun Ra's song "When There Is No Sun," go to https://youtu.be/4pHGXmwEaF4.

During our interview, my father told me a funny story about when he was traveling the road. He and some of his band members straightened their hair. Some styles were slicked close to the scalp while others were in a pompadour in front. Back in the day, it was a popular trend for Black men to straighten their hair. The chemical compound used to straighten the hair called conk had lye as a main ingredient. As the story continued, dad said, "Well, I put that conk on my hair. You had to let it sit for a while for it to straighten your hair. The curlier or thicker your hair, the longer you had to let it stay in your hair. I sat for a while, and it started to burn a little. I went to the bathroom sink to rinse it out. I kept turning the faucet, but no water came out. I started panicking. My scalp was really burning badly then. So I had to think quick, fast, and in a hurry. I saw the clear water in the toilet bowl and dunked my head in there so fast. I felt like I had to hurry up and rinse that conk out. My scalp felt like it was on fire. From that time on, I would always make sure the water was on when I straightened my hair with that conk."

Dad continued his memories about his travels and said, "So anyway, the next night, when we were playing at the Paradise Theater in Detroit, Prez was sitting out there in the audience. Duke Ellington was sitting in the audience too. You know he liked the ladies. He was sitting over there with about four or five ladies. Some say he was a player."

I asked, "Was he married?"

Dad said, "No, Duke wasn't married. So anyway, I was playing 'Body and Soul.'" Dad was singing the bars of the song. He made deep intonations in his voice. He was in the zone, making vocal sounds in the manner in which he played his horn that night. At that moment, he stopped abruptly and said, "You know while I was playing, Duke stopped talking to those ladies, turned around, and gave me a thumbs-up. He was so excited because earlier, he had told me that I needed to get my own tone. Duke came up on stage and said to me, 'That's it. That's it. That's it, kid. That's the tone I was talking about. Duke was so excited to play with us that he ran Sonny Blunt offstage and started playing piano with us. Al Hibbler was there, and he came up and sang."

I commented, "Oh, Al Hibbler was a singer?"

Dad said, "Yeah, he was a singer. We became friends too. I used to book him to sing out there on the road after

Duke died." My dad really knew what he was talking about and was not making stuff up. When he had gigs in Chicago after returning from being on the road, he'd have placards made to advertise. I came across one such placard while going through our house, looking for information for this book. This is one with a gig my dad had with Al Hibbler, who he mentioned during my interview with him.

I asked Dad, "Was Duke older than you?"

He said, "Yeah, Duke died in 1974. He was an old man."

I asked Dad if he knew Count Basie.

He said, "Yeah, I knew Basie. I worked with him for two weeks at the Fairmont Theater. When I was with Lil, we closed at the Apollo Theater. We had a couple of weeks off. So I worked with Basie at the Fairmont Theater in New York."

My dad has told me many stories about his travels as a musician in Lil Green's band. One such story happened when he was off the road and back in Chicago. He told a funny story about how one of the band members would snatch pay phones and take money from them. The musician had this activity as his "side racket" or "job." I thought that was hilarious. He also went on to tell me another story about a musician who had a book of his own musical compositions. Someone confiscated his book and was copying and playing his music while on the road. Things were as treacherous back then in the industry as they are now.

My dad gave a vivid detail of being off the road, away from the band. While off the road, he would go to New York and other cities. However, he also loved going back home to Chicago. This time, he was only going to be in Chicago for two weeks. Dad said that when he would go back to Chicago, he would always get himself a tripe sandwich. "Tripe is a kind of meat that consists of an animal's stomach lining. It may sound gross, but your tasty breakfast sausage may include a bit of tripe" (https:www.vocabulary. com). The tripe sandwich place was on the South Side of Chicago, on Prairie Avenue, right by an alley near Thirty-Fifth Street. He said those tripe sandwiches were very good. He got his sandwich to go. Then he went to the Grand

Terrace to eat his sandwich. That was when he met my mother, Marie Hazelwood.

Marie was at the Grand Terrace to rehearse with the all-girls band of which she was a member. Marie played alto sax. She learned how to play the clarinet when she was in high school. The all-girls band had just completed its rehearsal. My father noticed a lady from afar, standing at the back of the Grand Terrace, by the bandstand. She was talking to a man named Wanzo. He clearly remembered walking down this long hallway to the bandstand. When my dad got closer, he was stunned even more than he was when he first saw Marie from a distance. He said to himself, "Dang, who is that pretty woman there, boy!" So my dad went up to Wanzo and said, "Who is this fine lady? Aren't you going to introduce us, buddy?"

Wanzo turned to Marie and said, "This is Cozy Eggleston, with Lil Green's band, and he's home for two weeks."

Marie asked my dad, "Do you want to play with us?"

He said, "Yes."

That same day, Marie was with her niece Jackie, who lived with her. My dad asked Marie if he could walk them home, and Marie said okay. My dad walked them home and went home right afterward. My dad said, "It was on from there."

He began to rehearse with Marie at the old Armory where the soldiers went when off duty. The armory later became a church. Now it is renovated and a military school right across the street from my parents' home.

Dad reminisced about how, shortly after he met Marie, he would get a ride home with her and her boyfriend. He did not like the fact that she had a boyfriend because he liked her himself. Dad recalled how annoyed he would get because the boyfriend would make sure he got caught at the red light so he could steal a kiss from her. Once, when the same thing happened, Cozy told me he spoke up and said, "Man, why don't you go on and stop slowing up at the lights so you can get a kiss? We have to go on and get to work so we can be there on time, man. You are beginning to make me mad now. I just didn't want him kissing on her and stuff."

CJ's admiration for Marie grew stronger. Cozy couldn't hold back anymore. So one day, just on a whim, he told Marie to go and quit her boyfriend. While telling me the story, my dad said, "Do you know she came back and said, 'I just quit him!'?" Cozy continued and said, "I didn't think that she was really going to go and do that." He was in awe but very happy about it.

My dad also recalled how, right after Marie quit her boyfriend, he was walking down the street together with him. The now ex-boyfriend began to tell my dad that Marie had just quit him. My dad told him, "Oh really?" as if this was all news to him. My dad continued, "Her ex-boyfriend was pointing ahead to Marie and the drummer who was walking with her. The ex-boyfriend said, 'Look at him carrying Marie's horn. He must be the one she quit me for.'" My dad, in his unscrupulous manner, said to the ex-boyfriend, "The boy ought to be ashamed of himself to do you like that." My mom's ex-boyfriend had no idea my dad

44

was working him over and that he was actually the culprit, not the drummer. My dad was the one who took my mom from her ex-boyfriend. Afterward, it was time for CJ to hit the road with the band again. Cozy gave Marie a copy of his itinerary.

He remembered while back on the road right after he met Marie that she had a letter waiting for him in every city.

I asked my Dad, "What did the letters say? Were they love letters? Was she talking about how much she missed you?"

He blushed and said, "Yeah."

We burst out in laughter. He would also send her money to send to his mother, Mattie. She always sent the money to Cozy's mother. Cozy noticed that Marie was upholding him and his mother with her actions while he was on the road.

There was one time, though when he was perturbed in trying to locate her whereabouts by phone. He explained that the band was in Montgomery, Alabama, the Saturday before Easter. He called Marie. However, she was not at home. He said, "I called down there and said, 'Where in the heck is she at this time of night?'" He went on to say that her brother told him during the call that she had gone to work that night.

During our interview, my dad corrected himself and said, "No, it wasn't. It was in the daytime when I called. Her brother said she was at the beauty shop, getting ready for Easter." Dad stated that he was getting kind of mad about it. He later returned home to Chicago without Marie knowing. He said, "I went by her house, and she was not at home that Friday. I went up to the musicians' union building to holler at everybody. I began to wonder again why Marie was not at home. So that night, we were going to Thirty-Seventh and Vernon, to a place called the Off Corner Lounge. They jam over there at night. I saw Marie's cousin Ralph. We were going back over to the house at 3702, where Marie lived. The old man who she was working with was a drummer who had a band, and he drove up in front of the house. Marie got out of the car. I said, 'Hey, baby, how are you doing?' I was glad to see her boy." She was surprised and happy to see him too. Dad said, "We went on up to the house."

I asked him, "She let you come in there and stay with her, huh?"

He said, "Yeah, I did not sleep with her or nothing. I slept out there on the couch."

I broke out in laughter.

He continued, "So we got up and left early the next morning and went down to my house."

I probed further and asked, "What were you all doing, kissing?"

He said, "That isn't any of your business."

I asked him, "In what year did that happen?"

He said, "In 1946." He was getting a little uncomfortable with discussing these things with me as I was his daughter and all. But I kept pursuing with questions.

I asked, "What happened after that?"

He said, "Then later on, I moved in with Marie. We got married." He said he had gotten tired of the road and decided to go back to Chicago to be with Marie.

I asked him, "What year did all of that happen?"

He said in a huffy manner, "The same year, Connie!"

I said, "I'm just asking, Daddy."

He continued to say, "In 1946, sugar. All of the stuff I just told you about returning home unexpectedly occurred between January and April of 1946."

I told him that was a big step for him to leave Lil Green's band.

Again he said, "I was just tired of the road. I was thinking about Marie. I was just tired of the road."

They became husband and wife in June 1946. They had three children. My brother James came first, then me, and then my sister Rosemarie. James was born at Cook County Hospital. My sister and I were born at home at 3702 S. State Street, Chicago, Illinois. My dad described how I came before the doctor arrived.

He said, "Your mother was in labor with you at the house. She was so close to having you that we didn't have time to get to the hospital. So we called the doctor to come to the house instead. I was pacing and panicking, waiting for the doctor to arrive. Next thing I know, I heard a baby's cry. You came before the doctor could get there. He got there just in time to cut your umbilical cord and check you and your mother out. You both were just fine."

There's an old song—"Chicago"—by Fred Fisher that many singers sang, with lyrics saying, "On State Street that great a street, I just want to say, they do things that they never do on Broadway—say, They have the time of their life, I saw a man and he danced with his wife, in Chicago, Chicago, Chicago—that's my home town." I was born on State Street in Chicago. That's why I always sing these lyrics. My father had a son, Cletus Ray, in 1941—long before he met my mother. Cletus's mother's name was Willa Mae. She passed when Cletus was very young. His maternal grandmother, Mrs. Ray, took care of him. They lived in Cairo, Illinois, also. They were still living in Cairo when we moved there in 1951. I have fond memories of my brother Cletus. My grandmother would take my siblings and me to visit him. He told me that every time he'd see me, I would always smile from ear to ear. He continues to be an important part of my life.

I continued to probe Dad about leaving Lil Green's band. I asked, "How did you start your own band when you came off the road?"

He replied, "When I got ready to come home and leave Lil Green's band, I asked some of the band members to come back with me to Chicago. I told them we can go to Chicago to work."

I asked, "You conjured up enough members from the band?"

He said, "Yeah, they were in the rhythm section."

I asked, "Do you remember their names?"

He said, "Yeah, just three of them. Lindell Marshall was the drummer, Walter Jackson Johnson was the bass player, and Sonny Blunt was the piano player. We were all with Lil Green. We came home here to Chicago and started playing. All of them were from Chicago."

Cozy's Combo Band's Beginnings in Chicago

"When we got back, I asked the man who owned Club Evergreen, 'Can my band play there?' He hired me." Dad named his band—Cozy Eggleston and His Combo. The name Combo was popular then. Later in 1952, after he made his hit song "Big Heavy," he changed the name of his group to the Cozy Eggleston Band and Jazz Review. See the placard below.

Dad continued his story about his time working in Chicago after coming off the road with Lil Green and said, "We mainly worked on the north side. We worked on Cicero Avenue and Melrose Park, at all of the White clubs."

I asked, "Were you making pretty good money?"

He said, "Yeah, that's why I started working up north. I was working all over on the south side, but I got more money working on the north side."

Dad had an agent at that time, so I asked, "When did you get the agent?"

He said, "When I was with Lil Green, she had Joe Glaser out of New York as her agent. Joe Mussey was my agent at that time. Later, he booked me all over the United States."

I asked, "When did you start using the name Cozy?"

He explained, "When I came out of the army, I knew a guy named Cozy Cole. He was a drummer. I liked that name, Cozy, and I started to use it ever since then." Dad continued recalling his days back in Chicago after coming off the road. He said, "One day, when I went up to the musicians' union, I saw Lester Young or Prez, as they called him. Prez asked me, 'Who is that drummer you have with you?' I told him, 'That's Lindell Marshall.' Prez said, 'The guy plays nice.' I said, 'Oh yeah?'

"So your mother and I left from up there at the union that day. Prez fell down the steps and messed up his teeth. The next night, we came to work, and Prez was there. He asked me if I could fill in for him. So I filled in for him that night and for the rest of that gig. I did not charge him anything for filling in for him. That was Prez, my idol. I worked in his place for about three nights. At that time, your mother had a blond streak in her hair. Our friend Red had a blond streak too. Your mother changed her hair from blond to a red streak shortly thereafter. Your mother and I went over to the Beehive on Fifty-Fifth and Harper. Prez was there. He looked at your mother and said, 'Cozy, is that her? Is that her?' I said, 'Hey, man, what are you trying to do, get me in trouble or something? Yeah, that's her.'" Mom's change in hair color had Prez confused.

My dad continued, "So getting back to Lindell Marshall, my drummer, we played our set. When we got through playing our third set, Lindell came up to me and said, 'Cozy, I'm going to play with Prez.' I said, 'What?' I went to Prez and said, 'Hey, man, you've stolen my drummer, huh?' Prez said, 'The kiddy wants to go other places, Cozy.' I said, 'Okay, man, you know that's all right. I got another drummer for my band then.'"

I asked Dad what made him add Mom to his band.

He said, "I added her because I wanted another horn in my band. Also, I added her because I was going with her, and she played alto sax. I'd rather pay her than somebody else. She started working with me in 1946. That's when we got married." My dad explained to me that back in those days, booking agents frowned on husbands and wives playing in the same band. As good as my mother looked, my dad would've fought someone if they would've come after my mom. This would've stirred up a lot of trouble. Dad continued, "So we came up with a plan to get around the rules so she could be a band member. We created the name Marie Stone by taking the last four letters of our last name, *ston*, and placing the first letter of our last name, *E,* in back of that to form Stone.

Marie is my mom's middle name. Frances is her first name. So my mom became Marie Stone, playing alto sax in the band. This name-change idea enabled Mom to play and travel on the road in her husband's band.

During our interview, Dad talked about Joe Glaser. Later, while doing research on Dad's recounting, I came across an article mentioning Joe Glaser. The article verified his story. Glaser was a well-known manager in that era. The article discussed a very popular jazz club where famous jazz artists played. The name of the club was the Sunset Café—a pioneering jazz club dating to the 1920s—"became the Grand Terrace Café." The article continues and mentions the manager my dad talked about named Joe Glaser: "I'm also unclear when Louis Armstrong's manager Joe Glaser became owner of the club at 315—317 E. 35th Street" (Saith 2017).

It was amazing to find and read this article about the Grand Terrace. It was the place my father mentioned where he first met my mother. Later, the Grand Terrace became an Ace Hardware store in Bronzeville on Chicago's South Side. Our family lived within walking distance of the store. The store was on the corner of Thirty-Fifth and Calumet, and we lived on Giles, the next block over. The Meyers family took ownership of the club and named it Meyer's Ace Hardware. The store became a hot spot for the neighborhood residents in the Bronzeville community and the surrounding areas. Not only did the store have products essential to homeowners, but the Meyers gave advice. They would give suggestions on how to fix problems relating to plumbing and other related subjects.

Our family frequented there often. It was one of few stores to buy fuses that screwed into our fuse box at our house. The owners maintained much of the memorabilia left in the building from the Grand Terrace. They were jazz buffs and once told me they were very familiar with my parents as jazz musicians.

After serving residents in the Bronzeville area for over ninety-five years, the Meyer's Ace Hardware closed its doors on March 24, 2017. Now it's a beauty supply store. It was disheartening to see it go as it was an important fixture in the community.

12

Cozy Composing and Recording Music

Dad and I continued our discussion about his music. He continued, "First, with my band, I was playing everybody's tunes."

I asked, "When did you start composing and playing your songs?"

He said, "Later on, I put out a song in 1952 called 'Big Heavy.'" Cozy continued to write and compose songs for his band to play. Other songs in his repertoire included "Wham," "Moon Ray," and "Grand Slam." These songs became huge hits. Cozy continued to write and compose songs for his band to play. While going through some papers in our family home, I came across the original handwritten song of my dad's titled "No Business." The song was written on August 22, 1952, on original stationery from the Oakwood Manor Hotel, which was on 562-64 E Oakwood Boulevard, Chicago, Illinois.

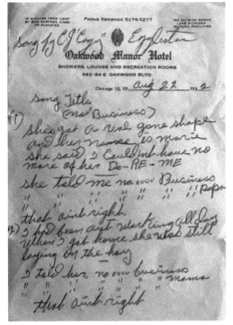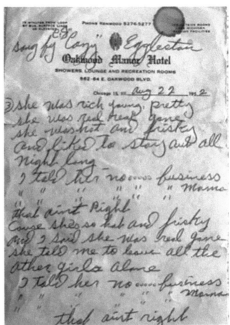

My siblings and I still lived in Cairo, Illinois, with our paternal grandmother—Grandma Mattie—at the time. When my parents returned to Chicago from being on the road, they would stay at the Oakwood Manor Hotel. My parents took my siblings and me to Chicago one summer, and we stayed with them at the Oakwood Manor Hotel. I will never forget what happened one day there.

My brother James and I had gone outside, in front of the hotel. He was ready to go back to the room, but I wasn't. I went back in and started wandering through the hotel, curious. When I decided to go back to our room, I realized I was lost and on another floor. My dad's band members would stay there too. I tried to find our floor but couldn't. That was when I started crying. I was around five or six years of age. Luckily, I was on the floor where my dad's band member was staying. My dad told me the band member's name was Boots. He heard me crying when he was inside his room, came out, saw who I was, and took me to my parents' room. I felt such joy when he rescued me from my frightful event. I never ventured around the hotel again.

My parents did some out-of-town gigs during that time too while living in Chicago. My maternal grand-mother, Ida Hazelwood, kept my brother and me while my parents were out of town. My mother was pregnant with my sister, Rosemarie, while she was traveling on some of those out-of-town gigs in 1951. She left the band to go back to Chicago to have my sister.

Cozy said, "I called home to see how the pregnancy was coming along. They told me that she was unable to come to the phone because she was giving birth to Rosemarie."

After my sister, Rosemarie, was born in 1951, he decided to keep his combo on the road.

I asked, "What made you stay on the go on the road?"

He said, "'Big Heavy' became a hit. I had composed it and sent it to Washington, DC, for copyright. I felt I could make more money from composing, recording, and playing my own songs than from recording somebody else's songs. I was with States Records then. I wrote 'Cozy's Beat' and got a copyright for it. After twenty-five years, I had to get a copyright for all my songs. But anyway, because I had a hit song, I decided to stay on the road. To really get your music out there during those times, traveling to different cities throughout the USA was the avenue. We could follow my hit and make a lot of money. But there was one huge problem. Who was going to take care of our three children, your brother James, your sister Rosemarie, and you, while we were on the road?"

As I pondered in my head, who else could it be except for my father's mother, Mattie, in Cairo, Illinois? My maternal mother, Ida Hazelwood, was a very young mother who left her children in the care of my maternal grandfather, Papa. So she definitely was not an option.

Dad explained, "Earlier, I had told my mother about my big hit, 'Big Heavy.' I had told her I needed to take my band on the road to really get paid. I was trying to get a feel for what she thought about it. I called my mother to ask her if she would be willing to take care of you all so your mother and I could go on the road. She told me, 'Well, you don't have anyone else to do it.' Then your grandmother said, 'Yes, I haven't raised any children since you, but I'll do the best I can.' She did a good job with the three of you."

I asked Dad how old his mother was at that time.

He went on to say, "She was born in 1897."

She was fifty-four years of age when she took my brother, my sister, and me into her home in Cairo, Illinois. I was three years of age going on four; my brother was four years of age, soon to be five; and my sister was just a baby at about two months old. This occurred in 1951.

13

My Cairo, Illinois, Memoirs

We went to live in Cairo, Illinois, in 1951. We called Dad's mother Grandma Mattie. My brother and I started attending Washington Elementary School. There was not a kindergarten program in Washington, so I entered school in the first grade. My brother, being sixteen months older, had already started there. I felt so secure with my big brother James, walking with him to school. I recall walking there on my first day. He told me to hurry because he didn't want us to be tardy. *Tardy* was a word unknown to me. I heard the word *toilet* and thought he was talking about the toilet. I thought, *What does that have to do with anything?* All kinds of things started going through my head—thoughts like *If we're late, are the teachers going to make us go to the bathroom and sit on the toilet for a while?* What changes young children go through in their minds with a mistaken word.

There was a neighborhood store named Johnnie's. All of the children would go there to buy candy. There was a long way to get to school and a shortcut. For the shortcut, we would walk on the side of Johnnie's store and cross over the railroad tracks. However, that was a way Grandma

Mattie did not want us to take. She felt that crossing the railroad tracks was too dangerous, but we took that short-cut anyway and a lot.

Since my grandmother had no girls, she did not know how to style my hair. She'd put it in these big clunky and ugly braids. I hated it so much I'd take them down before I entered school. My teachers would look at me in awe but never said anything to me about it. When I'd return home, my grandmother would ask me what happened to my hair. I'd tell her that it just came loose.

My grandmother was very strict with my sister and me. She was so overbearing on me that I came to the conclusion that she didn't like me at all. Since my sister was close to a newborn baby, my grandmother spoiled her often. She had given birth to my dad, a male. I guess she felt as if she finally had her own little girl.

We could barely go outside to play, but my brother could. So we made up a lot of games to play in the house. One such game was jumping off of the kitchen counter onto a small green stool. We had to jump onto the stool with precision to see who had the best landing. We got fancy with it. Once, I got real fancy with it—so fancy that I landed on the stool, broke it, and fractured my right foot. I remember a doctor coming to our house to look at my foot injury. He gave me a cane to use to walk until my foot healed. That happened one Easter. I had gotten all dressed up in my new Easter outfit and was walking around using a cane. As I got older, I noticed a small knot on the top of my right foot. As an adult, I asked my brother what happened to my foot. He told me I had broken it when I had jumped onto the stool. I'd always notice the knot on my foot but never knew I had broken it. I assume the doctor never put it in a cast. That's okay because the knot never impeded my movement in walking, jumping, dancing, or running.

As often as possible, my parents would make trips to Cairo to visit us when they came off the road. The feeling I got when I saw my parents was exhilarating. Whenever they came, they were always bearing gifts for my siblings and me. I recall getting an Annie Oakley outfit. For those who don't know, Annie Oakley was a sharpshooter. She became famous as part of the Buffalo Bill's Wild West show. Also, they gave my brother play guns with caps to make the popping sound. They would bring souvenirs to my grandmother from the various places they'd been while traveling. They were able to visit us sometimes for Christmas. They had gifts for us under the Christmas tree. Those were wonderful times as we didn't get to see our parents during the year.

My father, while I interviewed him, said, "While traveling on the road, we saw some real nice clothes. We purchased and sent them to you in Cairo for you to wear to school and to church. We didn't care how much they cost." That was when they bought me my favorite red velvet dress with white lace. I cherished that dress and was so upset when I outgrew it. My parents had very good taste. They dressed nicely, probably because they were entertainers. While traveling, they came across the latest fashions. We always dressed sharp. It became a family tradition. I definitely have happy memories of seeing my parents when they took breaks from being on the road to visit us.

Well, Grandma Mattie was still a very spiritual woman, as she was while rearing my dad. She took us to church every Sunday. I don't remember ever missing a Sunday at church unless someone was sick. She continued her ritual of cooking and taking meals to church, as she did while rearing my dad. We would stay after church to eat and socialize with other church members. As a young child, it seemed as if we were in church from sunup to sundown. I remember being in church, seeing my grandmother up, gyrating, throwing her hands up and all. Grandma Mattie was up in the choir, doing all of this. She was "shouting," as they do in the Baptist church. However, I was a young girl and didn't understand. I thought she was sick because of her actions and would always cry about it.

She would always sit us by this lady in church. One day, I understand, the lady told my grandmother about how I would cry as she shouted. So she started standing in the last row of the choir to hide from me so she could shout without me seeing her.

14

Cozy's Combo on the Road Again from 1951 to 1956

During my second interview segment, I said to my dad, "Do you know I've been taping our conversation?" I began interviewing Dad the next day and taping our conversation again on the recorder. I asked him, "How did your band travel when you were on the road?"

He said, "I had a Buick. I purchased it from Roger's Pontiac car dealership on Michigan Avenue. They're still there. I still do business with them. The father passed away. His son is there now."

I asked Dad, "How did you know how much to pay your band members?"

He said, "I paid my musicians based on the scale set by our local 208 musicians' union."

Facing prejudice while on the road: Jim Crow, civil rights

I asked him if they ran into prejudice while on the road.

He said, "Yeah, we'd run into prejudice." Dad recounted times when he and his band faced prejudice during their travels. My parents had just started a new gig then. He continued, "We played in Logansport, Indiana, on the other side of Gary."

I had never heard of the city, so I looked it up on the Internet. Well, there is a city in Indiana named Logansport located in Northern Indiana. It is near Indianapolis and Purdue University. Dad certainly had an excellent memory and was factual as usual in his recall. My father continued his story about his band playing in Logansport.

"We had played a session of our gig there, and it was time to take a break. During the intermission, the owner of the club asked me and my band to sit on the beer barrels in the back of the club to take our break. The club owner said, 'You and your band can't sit up front with the White crowd.' We were playing for them, but we couldn't sit with them. I told him that my band, especially my wife, was not going to sit on anybody's beer barrels in the back of this club."

"Do you see my wife's gown?" my dad asked. "I paid a lot of money for her gown, and she's not going to mess it up on any beer barrels. If we can't sit in the front, you can just give me my pay now, and we'll leave."

Then the club owner had a sudden change of heart. My dad and his band, including my mother, sat up front in the club. I assume the club owner wanted my parents to finish their set and not lose money. From that time forward, the owner had them sit by the window inside the club, up front.

My dad continued, "We sat in that spot in front of the window the next night during intermission. Black constituents from the community saw us and felt it was okay for them to come into the club. For the remaining time of our gig there, Black club goers continued to come watch us play. The club owner never told them to leave. He did not say a thing to his new Black constituents."

Also, he probably didn't want to lose any business. My parents turned segregation into integration, exclusion into inclusion, in that one instance.

Another incident occurred when my parents were playing in North Dakota. My dad said, "We went to the grocery store to buy some food. We were walking around in the store, looking. We were trying to find something good to eat to take back to the hotel. That's when I came across something that really caught my eye. I couldn't believe what I saw. I saw these cans of oysters on the shelf. I called Marie over and said, 'Look here. Do you see what it says on these cans of oysters?' They were called Nigger Head oysters. There was a Black man on them with bulging white eyes and large red lips in caricature. I noticed that the oysters were produced and shipped from Mississippi and distributed to a lot of White cities. I purchased some cans and brought them back to the *Chicago Defender* newspaper. They wrote an article about it and included a picture of the can, which they placed in their newspaper. *Jet* magazine also printed the story. When we went back up to North Dakota to play again, we went to that same store. They had taken all of those cans of oysters off the shelf."

I did some research on this myself to fact-check my dad's story. Here is a section I found in the *Jet* magazine about the canned oysters: "Name change of the week. Under repeated pressure brought by the NAACP, the Aughinbaugh Canning Co. of Biloxi, Miss., changed the name of its oysters. The old name: Nigger Head Brand. The new name: Negro Head Brand" (*Jet* magazine Vol. VIII, No. 15 August 18, 1955, A Johnson Publication 78 Ferris State University Jim Crow Museum, David Pilgrim).

Canned Mississippi oysters with new label.

15

Traveling on the Road with My Parents' Band An Adventurous Summer Vacation

One summer, my parents came to get us to travel on the road with them. It must've been the summer of 1956. My siblings and I were very young at the time, between five to nine years of age. I was seven years old, turning eight that coming October. I have fond memories of the summer my parents came to get us to travel with them. My dad, my mom, and his band traveled by car in a caravan across the country. My dad led the caravan in the Buick he mentioned in our interview. My parents and my siblings rode in the same car. The rest of the band members followed right behind in their cars. We were off on the long cross-country journey. I was told I'd fall asleep as soon as I got in the car to hit the road. I do remember traveling with them then and easily falling asleep. I tried, but I could never keep my eyes open. Sleep got the best of me.

I feel a surge of euphoria when I reminisce about those times. We'd travel many hours day and night, taking pit stops when necessary. My mom was an excellent driver and would take the wheel so my dad could sleep. My parents arranged places for us to stay prior to the trips. We'd stop and spend the night with relatives and friends. They lived on or near our travel route. During that time, there was a *Negro Travelers' Green Book*—a "travel guide published (1936–67) during the segregation era in the United States" (Wallenfeldt 2020). It listed businesses such as restaurants, drugstores, and hotels accepting African American travelers and was "compiled by Victor Hugo Green (1892-1960), a Black postman who lived in the *Harlem* section of *New York City*" (Wallenfeldt 2020). He wanted the guide to make it more comfortable and safe for African Americans to travel. The guide was available before the passage of the *Civil Rights Act of 1964.*

I don't remember if my parents used the *Green Book* during their travels when we were not with them. However, I do remember that while on the road with them, we once stayed with relatives who had a peach tree. They were really nice to us. They'd fix us breakfast and make us feel at home. My dad told me the relatives lived in Muncie, Indiana. My brother kept eyeing this particular peach that was not ripe yet but was very close to it. As soon as the peach was ripe, he pulled that peach off the tree and began to eat it. He devoured that peach. He did let us taste it too before he ate the whole thing. It was delicious. It was the juiciest and sweetest peach I'd ever tasted in my life.

While on the road, my siblings and I would do things to pass the time. We'd make up games to play. We'd count all the red cars, then all the white cars and so on. We would see a nice car and yell out, "That's my car!" We would watch the sun and say it was following us because it would be at that same spot no matter how many miles we traveled.

There were trials and tribulations along the way. I remember getting a flat tire. There were no towing companies or AAA roadside services then. My dad had to change the tire himself. My mother could change a flat tire too.

As we traveled that summer, little did we know that we were on our way to New York, where my parents had a big gig. My parents took us to Niagara Falls. My mom's sandal strap broke, and her scarf flew off into the misty air, swirling like a kite. This scene is so vivid in my memory. We crossed the border into Canada. I was so curious about the car lighter with the bright-red flame. So I placed my finger on it to see what it would do. Well, I found out and burned the tip of my finger. It wasn't a serious burn. My parents stopped and purchased some Bactine for my burn. Also, right after we crossed into Canada, I slammed my thumb in the car door while pulling it shut. My thumb was painful but not fractured. It seemed like something was always happening to me, but I would come out of it all right.

We made it to the hotel in New York where we were staying. It was a glamorous sight to see. The lobby was large with beautiful chandeliers. We checked in and made it to our room. My siblings and I loved our room, which was a suite with our parents' room separated from ours with a door. My parents were going to be on the radio that night. There was a radio in our room, so we could listen to them.

They were getting ready to go to perform at the club for the radio broadcast. My mom had on a very pretty gown.

She had a stunning collection of gowns to wear. She fixed her hair in various styles. Sometimes she would put red or blond streaks in her hair to change it up. One could tell she was an entertainer who knew how to woo a crowd. I thought she was the most beautiful woman in the world. My father had his male band members dress alike. They wore black tuxedos, a cummerbund around their waists, white shirts, and black bow ties. As the old saying goes, they were cleaner than the board of health.

We didn't go with our parents to that performance. We stayed in a room at the ritzy hotel. Our parents gave us specific instructions before they left. They turned the radio on to the station for us to listen to. My siblings and I gathered around the radio in anticipation of hearing our parents. It was such a treat to hear our parents on the radio while they performed at the club. We couldn't believe that we could hear them as they performed. Our eyes were big as we listened in awe. It was so awesome, an experience we'd always remember.

My sister, my brother, and I had fun while staying at the hotel that night. After listening to our parents, we saw those white fluffy pillows. That's when the fun began. We had a pillow fight, hitting one another with the pillows. We were really going at it with each other. When the fun ended, we sat there, looking at one another with fear on our faces. It was a sight for sore eyes. There were feathers all over the room. We knew we were in big trouble. Our world as we knew it was going to be over. We did not know what to do, so we just sat and waited in angst for our parents to return.

My parents came back to the hotel and saw those feathers all over the place. We just knew we were in for a serious scolding. However, the exact opposite happened. I guess they were so happy to have us with them that they didn't punish us. Instead, they made a deal with the maids. The maids were so nice; they told my parents they would clean it up. They gave the maids a big tip. The maids saved our hides!

The next evening, they were going to take us with them to the club. We were excited as we dressed in our best clothes. Once we entered the club, it looked somewhat small, not too big. It was a close, friendly, high-spirited environment. People were packed like sardines in the small cigarette-smoked-filled club. The crowd was in deep conversation with some people seated at reserved tables. Otherwise, it was standing-room-only in the famous club in New York. Listening to music played on the jukebox, people were laughing and dancing with beads of sweat dripping from their faces. They dressed in their finest clothes to go out to have a good time. They didn't care about the sweat. The club was a famous spot for club goers. If you didn't get there early, you probably would not have a chance to enter.

The jazz band was about to perform and the crowd waited anxiously. The club emcee introduced the band. It was none other than my dad and the great Cozy Eggleston's Combo, featuring my mom, Marie Stone. My dad's band consisted of a drummer, a bass player, an organ player, and my mom on the alto saxophone. My dad played a tenor saxophone. The crowd, still moving rhythmically, gathered around the bandstand, listening to the music.

We were definitely not old enough to be in the club with them while they played on the bandstand. But since we were their children, no one complained or said anything about it. I must've been between five to seven years of age. My siblings and I felt as if we were grown. It was such a wonderful feeling. They sat us at a small table stage left of the bandstand and within their sight. My parents ordered us 7UP with a cherry in it as if we had an alcoholic beverage. We sat there, sipping on our drinks, talking, and listening to our parents play as if we were adults.

The restroom was on the opposite side of where we were sitting. We had to walk in front of the bandstand to get to it. This would be my moment of fame. I recall getting up to go to the restroom as the band played. I walked across the floor in front of the bandstand. I vividly remember wearing my favorite red velvet dress with white lace on the bottom. It had a white petticoat under it to make it fuller. That's the dress my parents had gotten for me one Christmas. I was walking and prancing so the dress would swirl out in such a manner to bring attention to myself. I would get up every fifteen minutes and prance in front of the bandstand as if to go to the restroom. That was my moment of fame.

The Moon Glows, a group billed as an act at the same time as my parents, performed on stage that night. My brother, who loved to sing, had so much fun meeting the Moon Glows. They even let him come up on the bandstand with them. "The Moon Glows were discovered in Cleveland, Ohio, in 1952 by legendary disc jockey Alan Freed… They achieved national fame after signing with *Chess Records* in 1954. On such successful records as "Sincerely" (1954)… The Moon Glows were inducted into the *Rock and Roll Hall of Fame* in 2000" (Pruter 2014).

The song, written by Harvey Fuqua and Alan Reed and published in 1954, is from the doo-wop era. It was number 1 on the R and B chart. Members of the Moon Glows singing "Sincerely" included Harvey Fuqua, Bobby Lester, Alexander "Pete" Graves, Prentiss Barnes, and Billy Johnson on guitar. To hear their hit song "Sincerely" (1954), go to https://youtu.be/BTIERquza6Q.

◊ **Coolin' It With Cozy:** Teaming up with bandleader Cozy Eggleston, alto saxophonist Marie Stone blows some "cool" jazz to the delight of youthful patrons in a Chicago night club. Eggleston, whose five-piece band tours the Midwest, says Miss Stone "blows real crazy."

To listen to Cozy Eggleston's "Big Heavy" (1955), go to https://youtu.be/ZQNCxX_RAQP8I.

Unlike our childhood experience in the small populated city of Cairo in Southern Illinois, we found some really nice White friends while staying at the hotel. We used to meet in the hotel lobby and venture through to check out the sights. Once, my sister and I were sitting outside, in the car, when it started raining. Our friends came to the car with their umbrellas to rescue us from the rain. I didn't get out to go with them; but my sister, who is three years younger than me, accepted the offer. She hadn't started school yet and not had experienced segregation, as I had. I wasn't used to having White friends in Cairo, Illinois. There was a stark difference in race relations in the north—in that hotel environment—as opposed to my experience in Cairo, in the south. Despite my one encounter, not accepting the umbrella offer, my brother, my sister, and I still have fond memories. We will never forget our summer trip to New York with our parents and the friends we met.

16

An Event to Change Our Lives Forever

During an interview segment with my dad, he recalled that his band, Cozy's Combo, was playing in Milwaukee, Wisconsin. He said, "We were playing on the bandstand when my sister-in-law and brother-in-law walked into the club. I said to the crowd, 'My in-laws just walked in. They came all the way from a Chicago to see us play.'" Dad explained, "I was on the bandstand, playing, and I saw Preston and Amanda coming into the club. But they didn't look happy. I noticed that they had solemn looks on their faces. That's when they told me about my mother's stroke. They came to tell me my mom, Mattie, had a stroke while at church in Cairo."

I remember that day vividly. One Sunday, while in church, Grandma Mattie had a stroke. I said at that time to my siblings, "See, I told you Grandma Mattie was sick." I can still see them carrying my grandmother out of the church. Some church members took us home. I also remember standing at the door and seeing my grandmother lying in bed in her room. She could only stare. The stroke took her speech and mobility. There was so much chaos in the house. Church members looked through drawers and scrambled through the house to find contact information on my parents' location. I didn't recall at the time how they found my parents, but they did find them. Later I found out our neighbors had found my aunt Amanda and uncle Preston's phone number. They called to tell them about my grandmother's stroke. My uncle and aunt were the ones who went to Milwaukee to tell my parents about my grandmother's stroke.

As the story goes, because I vaguely remember, my dad sent his stepsister to care for us until my mother could get to us. Dad's stepsister may have been in her twenties. I remember her being there. She only stayed a couple of days or so and left us to fend for ourselves. As previously mentioned, at that time, my brother was eight going on nine, my sister was four going on five, and I was seven going on eight. I remember being so afraid. But my brother, James, consoled my sister and me as best as he could. He was a strong role model for us during those times and even later in life. The neighbors took care of us after dad's stepsister left us. Also, my dad had his relatives from Tennessee come to take care of us until my mother could get there. Mom left the band and came to Cairo. Dad stayed on the road to finish the job in Milwaukee as he was on contract. This all occurred in 1956. To this very day, I shy away from any church, Baptist in particular, whose members shout. If someone shouts when I attend church, it brings back memories from that horrible day of my grandmother's stroke. I think shouting is the culmination of the sad songs and the preacher's sermon, which invokes sad feelings in people. That's my opinion, however, because of my experience with my grandmother. I still have the vision of members carrying her out of the church. So later in my adult life, I became a member of and joined a Presbyterian church. I enjoy the peace and serenity. I know this is for me. There are enough struggles and sadness in life as it. Church should be a place to give us peace, happiness, and solitude. As the saying goes, to each his own. No offense to how people practice religion. People are free to do as they wish.

Moving the Family
Back to Chicago (1956)
My Childhood Memories

We all moved back to Chicago that year in 1956. We lived and started school in the same neighborhood where my parents met and lived on the South Side of Chicago. Now it is known as Bronzeville, a historic district. "Bronzeville is a center for African American life and culture in Chicago. Historically known as the city's 'Black Metropolis,' Bronzeville had a strong sense of pride in its influential history and cultural scene…the annual Bud Billiken Parade, the nation's largest African American parade, which draws more than one million spectators each August" (Chicago, Choose Chicago, Neighborhood Bronzeville 2022).

Here is a picture of me in the Bud Billiken parade, taken by my dad.

During my interview with my father, he talked about seeing Lester Young (the Prez), meeting my mom, and playing in his band. It all happened in Bronzeville. I understand that currently, a company is pushing to build a gambling casino in Bronzeville. Many residents who live in the historical district do not want a casino there. Many say it will hurt existing businesses and bring more crime to the historical district. I tend to agree.

Chicago was certainly different from Cairo. We received an excellent education in Cairo. Since it was a quick transition to leave Cairo and move to Chicago, our family moved in with our maternal grandmother, Ida Hazelwood. We called her Hazelwood. She had a Native American lineage. My mom told us it was Blackfeet Indian. I remember her long black hair. Also, I remember my mother telling me that her mom, Ida, would color her hair with black coffee. My maternal grandmother would place her hair on an ironing board and straighten it with an iron. Her home was in the Bronzeville neighborhood, in the 3600 block on Giles Avenue. My mom told us that when she was a small child, her mother left her and her two brothers in Batavia, Illinois. She left them with her father, Richard Hazelwood. Her mother moved to Chicago. According to my mom, her parents married when her mom, Ida, my maternal grandmother, was still playing with dolls. So my grandfather Richard Hazelwood was much older than my grandmother Ida.

Later, my parents found us an apartment at 3650 S Calumet Avenue, and we moved out of our grandmother's house. The apartment was one block over from my grandmother's house, from Giles Avenue to Calumet Avenue, and was still in Bronzeville.

We moved back to Chicago during the summer months. So my parents had time to find us a good school to attend. Plus, Bronzeville is the same neighborhood my parents lived in before they went on the road with their band. So they were very familiar with the area.

There were two grammar schools in the area. They were the Wendell Phillips and Raymond grammar schools. My parents researched the better schools in the neighborhood, and the Wendell Phillips grammar school came out on top. However, families residing north of Thirty-Seventh Street, in the 3600 block, had to attend Raymond Elementary School. Those living in the 3700 block had to attend Wendell Phillips. We were zoned for Raymond. Since we lived in the 3600 block, my parents had to fudge a little bit of our address so we could attend Wendell Phillips. So we fudged our address to 3750 to attend Wendell Phillips. The school administrators weren't as strict back then regarding the proof of residency. Parents didn't have to show proof of residency. They didn't require a copy of a utility bill or anything of that nature back in the day.

I remember not being old enough to start third grade because my birthday was in October. However, the grades on my report cards were so high that I was able to start third grade and not repeat second grade. In recollection, the neighborhood children were in awe of all of the As and Bs on the report cards I received attending school in Cairo, Illinois.

I started third grade. The fudge worked, but I remember in third or fourth grade, my teacher asked me where I lived. I mistakenly gave my teacher my correct address. I blurted out my correct address, and the teacher had this strange look on her face. I really didn't know that my parents had fudged our address in order to attend Wendell Phillips. I remember the look on the teacher's face. However, I believe that because I was such a good student, she definitely let it pass. I completed the rest of my grammar school time through eighth grade, graduating in June 1962.

I have some good memories of growing up on the block at 3650 Calumet Avenue. I remember my sister, my brother, and I walking to our grandmother Ida Hazelwood's house. We called her Hazelwood. As previously mentioned, she was of Native American descent, a Blackfoot Indian, according to my mom. When my sister and I visited her, we would dress up our dolls, put them in our baby buggy/stroller, and push it in the snow. My maternal grandmother was a strict disciplinarian. Her nerves would be short with my brother, my sister, and me. Whenever we did something or behaved in a way she didn't like, she told us to line up and sit on her couch. She took a wire hanger and gave each of us one light whack. It was more frightening than anything. Later in my adult life, I remember telling my dad about the hanger discipline. He told me we should've told him about it. My grandmother passed away when I was around eleven years old. I remember my parents sneaking us into the hospital to see her. We weren't old enough to visit, according to hospital regulations. I can vividly remember combing my grandmother's long black hair, with some strands of gray, during the hospital visit. That was my last time seeing her alive. She passed a few days later. The year was 1960. I was eleven years old. Ever since then, I disliked hospitals and blamed them for her death. I hated hospitals for a long time because of it. That was my young mind going to work then. I didn't understand at the time.

I remember the fights we had in our new block on Calumet. Growing up in Chicago, when you're the new kid on the block, other children approached you. They wanted to see what you're made of. If you didn't fight, you'd get beat up or picked on the whole time you lived in that neighborhood. I knew my parents weren't going to move anytime soon because we had just moved there. So we fought back. Also, our dad told us that if we didn't hold our ground and fight back, he'd have a whipping for us afterward. We didn't want him to get that belt out. We were all afraid of that belt. He had a special belt for us—his favorite. We hid that belt so he couldn't find it. It was a thick belt. He'd get a thinner belt when he couldn't find his favorite one. Anyway, the fighting didn't stop, but we passed the initiation. The cycle continued whenever new kids moved into the neighborhood. They either passed initiation, or they didn't. I remember one family moved away because of it.

We played outside a lot in those days. There were no cell phones, iPads, or video games. We played hide-and-seek; jump rope; and catch a girl, kiss a girl. In this game, the boys would give the girls a time limit to run. When that time was up, the boys would chase us. They'd chase the girl they wanted to kiss. When the girl was caught, she'd have to give the boy a kiss. Well, my dad was so strict that all of the boys in the neighborhood were afraid of him. So they'd run past me. Plus, I think they wanted to catch the more mature, voluptuous girls—the ones they knew who'd give them a kiss. I was really skinny back in those days. With my dad in the back of my mind, I sure wasn't going to give up any kisses. It's funny, though. I sure was out there, playing the game.

We loved going to the neighborhood store to buy white potatoes. My friends and I would select the best potato we could find. We'd inscribe our names on our potato. We baked our potatoes by digging a hole in the dirt in the ground, starting a fire, and placing it in the fire to cook. That was new to my siblings and me, but we caught on really quick. Those baked potatoes sure tasted good. Another game we played outside was hopscotch. We'd draw adjoining squares on the sidewalk using chalk. Each square had a number from 1 to 9, with a 10 at the top we labeled in sky blue. We'd throw an object of our choice first on number one. We had to hop over the number 1 and hop on one foot to the other numbers ahead. We hopped until we reached the sky blue. I loved using colored chalk to draw hopscotch on the sidewalk. Coloring sky blue, drawn in the shape of a cloud, was my favorite.

My neighborhood friends and I were business-minded too. We ventured beyond the lemonade stand. A group of us would ask our parents for money to buy items to sell. We sold hot dogs, chips, and candy. We made a good profit too.

We played outdoors a lot. We'd purchase spinning tops, Hula-Hoops, jacks, horseshoes, Bolo bats, and marbles. We would try to collect the prettiest marbles money could buy. We traded them too. We played the game of mumblety-peg. In this game, we used a knife and threw it into the ground, in the dirt. The object of the game was to see who had the best stick/throw. Players could knock another player's knife over. Also, they could stick their knife as close as possible to one of the opponents. We played other games such as follow-the-leader; Red Rover; and red light, green light. We played softball and two-hand-touch football in the neighborhood's vacant lot.

I was so athletic and good at sports. The boys would let me play softball and two-hand-touch football with them. With me considered a true tomboy, the boys would let one other girl in the neighborhood play. We were the only two girls the boys would let play softball and other sports except for basketball. That was the only sport off-limits for girls. Their basketball court was sacred and only for them. I wasn't a true tomboy. I played with dolls with my girlfriends. We'd dress them up in various outfits. One Christmas, my parents bought me this huge, life-size baby buggy. We'd have fun, pushing my baby buggy through the neighborhood block. There was one friend residing in our neighborhood who came premature at birth. We would put her in the large buggy as if she was a baby. She'd make baby sounds too. We fooled a lot of people.

Double Dutch was the girls' favorite game. "Double Dutch is a forgotten Black community staple that goes back thousands of years. 'Rope skipping' was done in Ancient Egypt and China and eventually Europe. *Dutch colonists brought the two-rope version over to America in the 1600s*, which is why it's called 'double Dutch.'…two persons, holding ends…swing them back and forth…for one or two others to jump over" (Jones 2019; https://www.dictionary.com).

For those who may not know, it's played with rope. It's the same rope on which our mothers used to hang clothes to dry after washing them. We'd always run races to see who was the fastest one in the neighborhood too.

A group of our neighborhood friends would get money together to go to the neighborhood movie theater. The Louis Theatre—located at 108 E. Thirty-Fifth Street, Chicago, Illinois 60616—was in our neighborhood in Bronzeville. It was within walking distance. To get there quicker, we used a shortcut: jumping a fence in the alleyway. Another famous theater in Bronzeville was the Regal. My parents did allow us to go there with our friends. We'd catch a jitney to get there. The jitney was a popular mode of transportation in Chicago's South Side in Bronzeville.

"Decades before Uber and Lyft, taxis operated outside municipal regulations are called jitneys, named from a slang expression for a nickel, the original fare…jitney cabs, in Chicago the phrase for most of the 20th century referred to cars that worked the South Side and operated like busses on a set route" (Grossman 2014).

The Regal Theater—located at 4719 S. Dr. Martin Luther King Jr. Drive, Chicago, Illinois 69615—was about ten blocks up the street called South Park Avenue at that time. The street name changed to Martin Luther King Drive in honor of the slain civil rights leader. We shortened the name to King Drive. An article contributed by Ray Martinez and Bryan Krefft gives information on the theater's beginning: "The Regal Theater, which opened in 1928 as part of a huge real estate development in the heart of Chicago's historic Bronzeville." Upon entering, the theater was a beautiful sight to see: "The ceiling of the auditorium was designed to look like a huge canopy sputtered on the side walls with poles gilded in gold and… Middle Eastern landscape between the poles." The article continues, stating that it was "equipped with a state-of-the-art ventilation system, dressing rooms, an orchestra pit, and a Wurlitzer organ." The Savoy Ballroom was on the same block as the Regal Theater on South Parkway in Bronzeville. The area became known as, "the Harlem of Chicago for its important cultural and social contribution to the African-American community in Chicago." There were many stores in that area too. There were major shoe, jewelry, clothing, and department stores. My parents would always take my siblings and me shopping there. One other important point that the article notes is the hiring practices at the Regal. The developers, Lubiner & Trinz, unlike others, "staffed its flagship palace with mostly African-American management, ushers, house musicians, cashiers, and attendants. Most other major Chicago theaters at the time would only hire African-Americans for janitorial and behind-the-scenes jobs" (cinematreasures.org).

Not only did the Regal Theater show movies, but a lot of African-American jazz greats performed there. Famous jazz artists who performed there include Count Basie, Billie Holiday, Ella Fitzgerald, and Duke Ellington. Once, my parents took my siblings and me to see the famous blues artist B.B. King. We entered the theater and watched; however, that wasn't our type of music. So we kept getting up and leaving to go to the lobby. We stayed out there for as long as we could. When we attended the performances there, we went to see the R and B groups. I remember watching the Motown group called the Temptations there. My sister and I would swoon over them. We'd pick out the one we thought was the most handsome and our favorite. After their performance, they would throw souvenirs into the audience. When the Temptations completed their performance, my heartbeat, Eddie Kendrick, took his cuff link off. He threw it into the audience, and guess who caught it? I did. People sitting around me were so envious. That moment was so exhilarating. I don't know where the cuff link is to this day, but I cherished that cuff link for years.

The Regal Theater, Forty-Seventh Street, Chicago, Illinois

My father was a father figure to many children in the neighborhood. He'd load up our white station wagon and take our neighborhood friends to the Thirty-Fifth Street beach. He'd let them get on top of his shoulders to jump into the water as if they were on a diving board. He'd take our family to this place called Riverview. It was a popular amusement park in Chicago during those times. It opened in 1904 and closed in 1967. There was a scary roller-coaster ride called the Bob. One felt the wrath while sitting in seats in the front. My father and my brother did, but I never sat in the first row. There was also a ride where you'd stand against a round wall. It would spin around, and the floor would move down, leaving you nothing on which to stand. I guess the speed of the spin kept us attached to the wall. I think we did have to put a safety belt around us. There was also a room that had people who could do strange things. I saw a man who could pop his eyes out of his sockets. Also, there were contortionists. There were games to win toys and good food to eat. I loved the cotton candy. We loved when our parents took us to Riverview.

There were neighborhood block parties for children residing in the 3500 to the 3600 on Calumet Avenue. Adults in the neighborhood would sponsor the event and have hot dogs and other food for us. The city of Chicago provided the sponsors with large yellow wooden "horses" to keep traffic from entering our block. They were made of a long piece of wood on top with two triangular pieces attached to each end. The block parties were held during the summer months. My parents purchased summer outfits for us to wear each year for the outdoor block party. This was a highlight for all of my friends. We'd strut around, showing off our new outfits and shoes like a fashion show. We had so much fun at those annual block parties. Those were the good ole days.

There was one scary incident that happened while living on 3650 Calumet Avenue. It was a four-story apartment building. There were eight families, with two on each floor. My father was away on a gig but in the city. Our apartment was on the right side of the fourth floor. My mom, my siblings, and I were watching TV. All of a sudden, we heard loud banging on our door. A man was banging on our door in a rage. He was saying someone was after him. He ran up the flight of stairs in our four-story building. Since our apartment was on the last floor on the right, he had nowhere else to escape. He was banging on our door so hard. We thought he was going to break our door down. My mom ran to the closet where my dad kept his hunting rifle. She stood, holding the rifle, aiming squarely at the door as we huddled behind her in fear. My mother was not tall in stature. It appeared the rifle was bigger than her. She held it tightly and did not flinch. She was not afraid. She was ready to pull the trigger to protect her children and herself. She was a brave woman at that moment, unyielding. She didn't have to shoot anyone because after a while, there was silence. The man went away. I don't know to this day what happened to him, but he wasn't at our door anymore.

Later, while in high school, we moved to 3652 Giles Avenue, which was one block over. We moved again later in 1966 when my parents purchased a house at 3548 S Giles. I was going to graduate from high school that summer. My dad told me the story of how he was able to buy the house.

He said, "Every day, while walking up the street to the neighborhood grocery store, I'd see this beautiful house. It was such a nice place. One day, I saw this man on the front porch of the house. It looked as if he was fixing up the house. I kept asking him about the house every time I walked by. One day, he finally told me he was fixing up the house to sell it. He told me he was selling his house because he was a physician and ready to retire. I explained to him I was a musician with a family, just coming off the road with my band. I told him how we had saved up money to buy a house but used it to care for my mother, who had a stroke. He had empathy for me as I told him I couldn't buy the house straight-out. He told me that he would set up a monthly plan for me under one condition. The condition he gave was for me to keep the house in good condition."

I asked my dad what happened next.

He said, "You know, Doc would come by every now and then. He really wanted to see if I was true to my word of keeping the house in good condition. He'd come and look around downstairs and even go upstairs. He'd have a smile on his face, showing satisfaction. Once, when he came by, I was just about to fix up some things on the house. He had this worried look on his face like dissatisfaction. I told him I was in the process of fixing it. He came by later after I fixed the problems, and he had that smile on his face again. After a while, he stopped coming by the house. We burned the deed later on, down the line."

I remember when they paid the final payment on the house. My parents were so happy and proud.

Dad continued, "Your mother and I had saved a lot of money while on the road, with a goal to buy a house. However, to care for my mother after her stroke, we used most of our savings. I had given my mother money to get health insurance when she was caring for you all, but she didn't get any. She was my mother, and your mom agreed to use our savings to care for her after her stroke. So there went our dreams of buying a house for our family. It was the day I saw the man on the front porch at 3548 that was a catalyst. He helped make our dream of homeownership come true."

Once, Dad had gotten a gig for his band. The gig was in Chicago, not too far from our home. My mom was getting dressed to get ready to go play the gig they had gotten for the band. My sister and I would always watch as she made herself beautiful for the stage performances. Like most female entertainers, she would come up with these extravagant looks. She'd dye a blond or red streak in her hair using a mixture consisting of hydrogen peroxide. One day, my sister and I put some in our hair to get a streak too. It didn't come out too light because we didn't know what we were doing. Mom wore the most beautiful clothes. Some were gowns, and others were a different array of designer clothes and jewelry. My mother could sew, and she sparked an interest in me to take a sewing class. I became so good at sewing that I made my mother a form-fitting gold-looking long gown with a slit and a bow. The bow, made of peau de soie material, went across the top of the dress from one shoulder strap. It slanted down near her armpit where there was no strap. I felt so proud, seeing my mom wear the dress I'd made for her to wear on stage.

18

Cozy and His Band Back in Chicago Again (1956)

I have wonderful memories of my childhood upon returning to Chicago in 1956. I lived in Cairo for five years of my early childhood, from 1951–1956. I was age three and under the care of Grandma Mattie in 1951. I was age seven going on eight in the upcoming month of October when my parents moved us back to Chicago in 1956. Returning to Chicago was the beginning of a new chapter in my life. I was going to be able to see the life of my parents as musicians firsthand.

My siblings and I had a fierce interest in music, song, and dance. We were living in the era of '60s music, especially Motown sounds: the Supreme, the Temptations, Stevie Wonder, the Four Tops, Martha Reeves and the Vandellas, Smokey Robinson and the Miracles, Gladys Knight and the Pips, and the Temptations, just to name a few. When my parents purchased our first console with a radio and a turntable, we were elated. We were able to go to the neighborhood record store named Norman's and buy singles of popular songs we'd heard on the radio. At the time, there was a song put out in 1961 by the group the Marcels called

"Blue Moon." We loved that song. It was a number 1 international hit on the Billboard 100 chart. One time, my siblings and I put up an argument with our parents on how the song "Blue Moon" was the only version made. We put up a valiant fight, thinking we were correct. They proved us wrong. They pulled up information from the encyclopedia, as there was no Google at the time. "'Blue Moon'… was initially a popular tune from the 30s, composed by Richard Rodgers with lyrics by Lorenz Hart in 1931. There have been many different versions done by various artists, including the Marcels, Chris Isaak, Nat King Cole, Elvis Presley, Billie Holiday, Frank Sinatra, Dean Martin, the Mavericks, Glenn Miller, and Rod Stewart" (Fox 2013). After they set us straight, our jaws dropped. How could we think we knew more about music than they did? And they were jazz musicians. We were referring to the version of the song sung by the doo-wop group the Marcels. This version was popular on the music charts in the early '60s. I was an early teen at that time. You know sometimes youngsters of the newer generation think they know more than those in the older generation.

Continuing my interview with Dad, I asked him about his career in music after returning to Chicago in 1956. I asked him where he played.

He said, "North side. I played everywhere. I played out in Melrose Park. I can't think of the name of that club that was in the basement. I played all over the city everywhere. I was playing out in Elgin."

I remember Dad also played at a club on the north side called the Bowery. It was in the basement. The club

93

had peanuts in a shell on the tables for its customers to eat. They could throw the shells on the floor. He took us by there once to show us where he worked, but we weren't old enough to enter. Also, they played at the Trocadero Lounge/Club, which was on 4719 S Indiana Avenue, Chicago, Illinois. The Fox Motel occupies the space now.

Dad told me another story—not funny but a serious one. He said, "My band had a gig at this nightclub. We were playing on stage. All of a sudden, someone came in and started shooting up the place. I don't remember the name of the place. They weren't there to harm band members." He continued in an eerie tone, "We stopped playing immediately. I ran toward the back of the club by the kitchen. I was trying to get out of there so bad I tore the hinges off the cafeteria door. I ran outside and jumped a fence to get away from danger." Later he had to go down to the police station to discuss the incident. They cleared my dad and his band members, who had nothing to do with the shooting incident. I remember when that happened. He was very solemn when he arrived home that night. I never found out what happened after that.

I have fond memories of acting as a secretary for my dad. He asked me to help him identify members to play in his band. We had a small chair with a telephone on top. There was a section under the phone to place the Chicago directory of city residents: the white pages. Additionally, there was a yellow page for businesses. There was a directory of union musicians published by Local 208. I became very familiar with the Local 208 directory and used it to call musicians to offer them positions in my dad's band for gigs in the city. I had that responsibility for a while and felt as if I really knew those musicians personally. My father gave me a little stipend to work as his personal secretary. That was a fun job.

Another place my father had gigs was at Club Delisa in Chicago's South Side, on Fifty-Fifth and State Street. It was owned by the Delisa brothers, who were Italian Americans. They set it up as a prominent spot for African Americans. The Cotton Club in New York was a "Whites only" club, and Black bands could only perform there. Unlike the Cotton Club, Club Delisa's owners promoted an integrated crowd.

While explaining his story to me, I asked, "What year did you start your record label?"

He said, "I started my record label in 1969, but I didn't do anything with it until 1971. I recorded in 1971." He understood and completed the process to get his own label.

I asked, "What is the first album you put out?"

He continued, "*Grand Slam*. I had a baseball diamond on it, and I was sitting in the center, at the pitcher's mound."

I asked, "What was the name of your second album?"

He answered, "*Whammin & Slammin*."

I asked, "What was on that album?"

He replied, "What do you mean?"

I responded, saying, "You had some of your hits on those albums, didn't you?"

He said, "'Wham' was my hit. 'Nearness of You' was a hit. 'Sweet Merri Dee,' the radio DJ Merri Dee made it famous for me, made it a hit. She kept playing it all of the time. She was a very good friend of mine." She was a local radio disc jockey.

I continued and inquired about the coverage he had on the Internet and how he found out about it. He recounted a story about his friend Jody Christian and said, "A friend of mine came by here, Jody Christian, a piano player. He made records. He told me to go get on the Internet. He pulled up my name to show me stuff that was about me." Dad went on to say, "I didn't know I was on the Internet. He came by here and turned on my computer. Boy! I'm on Yahoo, Barnes & Noble, and all the records that I was on with other people."

I asked him, "What was the name of the record label?"

He said, "My band was on States Records. I'm talking about the records I was on with other artists. Now, like in 1946 or 1947, I did a session with Jump Jackson and other artists around here. Jump Jackson was the leader of this band. I sang on these records. I sang 'Grunt Meat Blues,' 'Farmer's

Daughter Blues,' and 'Are You Getting Married, Brother.' It was something like Louis Jordan's song 'Beware.'"

As he sounded off those names, I thought, *Listen to those names. Those are some kinds of names for songs. What kind of songs could they be, and what in the world does it sound like?*

Dad continued his story. "We did all of those records."

I asked, "Wasn't it on an album?"

He recalled, "We were called the Memphis Seven on some of them. We were called the Chicago All Stars on some of them. We were recording for Columbia Records. Melrose was in charge of getting the talent for Columbia. At that time, I was doing quite a bit of recording with other artists. So I sang. I did all of the singing in the band."

I intervened and said, "Didn't you play your saxophone on some of them too?"

He said, "Yeah, I played on them, but I was the singer. Then that's when I started... I was playing around the city here, you know."

I was trying to get my dad to remember this other album he was on. I was calling out a name and asking him for a name.

He said, "That was the masters of United Records. Bob Koster bought the masters. After Allen died, Smitty sold all of those masters to Bob Koster. He has a record shop downtown." He said that Bob Koster told him, "Cozy, I bought your masters because it was a big hit when I went out east to Buffalo, New York." Then at that moment, Dad broke into his storytelling mode. He asked, "Did I tell you about how they were using my music as a theme song?"

I told him to go on and explain.

He started telling me about Allen Freid, who was a big-time man. He had Li'l Richard and all of them in movies, traveling on tours. He went on to say, "Freid was on the radio, WIND, in Buffalo. I recorded with Leonard Allen under my own name. George "Hound Dog" Lorenz, the DJ, was using my song 'Big Heavy' as a theme song for years."

While searching the Internet and looking for the disc jockey Hound Dog, I was able to find information on him. George Lorenz, later known as Hound Dog, was born in October 1919. Later in life, in 1955, he became a DJ for WKBW radio in Buffalo, New York. The Hound Dog ended his show…with the Hound Dog howl carrying into his theme song, "Big Heavy"—a song from my dad's album.

My dad continued, "When Hound Dog retired, he put my tune 'Big Heavy' in the Musical Hall of Fame."

I recall when my father went to New York to obtain his royalties from all those years Hound Dog used his song "Big Heavy" as a theme song. He sued Bob Koster to get his master's. He succeeded. There are many things I can say about my father. I know one thing for sure: he goes after whatever it is to attain his goal. To hear a clip of my dad's song "Big Heavy," used as a theme song by Hound Dog to open his radio program, visit https://youtu.be/3L47KT-RTnk. One can see in the comment section that people truly love my parents' music.

That evening, while interviewing my dad, I sat on the floor, snuggled up next to him. He was sitting up comfortably in his recliner. I was having so much fun, interacting with him.

He continued talking about his music and traveling days, and said, "My band went to Buffalo, New York. We played out there. You were with us. I took you all [meaning my brother and sister] with us one summer. We played at the Zanzibar."

I began to reminisce about that time. I remembered being in the hotel, listening to my parents playing on the radio. I remember being in the hotel, listening to our parents on the radio in our hotel room. I can't forget the pillow fight with my siblings and getting feathers all over the hotel room.

He continued to discuss the one album he was on called *Honkers & Bar Walkers* and said, "The man who had the music for that album used the tunes of the artists he had on his label and other labels. It's on the Internet, and my albums are on there too. A lot of my music is on YouTube. He put my two records on there…on the album, and called it *Honkers & Bar Walkers*."

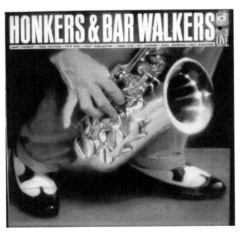

I recall visiting home while both of my parents were still living. My parents gave me a copy of the CD *Chicago Jump Bands, Early R & B Vol. I, 1945–1953.* I listened to my father sing, from years earlier, on the CD with a very young-sounding voice. The titles of the songs had me flabbergasted. He sang a song on the CD with the Chicago All Stars named "Are You Getting Married, Brother." Here is an excerpt from the inside cover of the *Chicago Jump Bands* CD: "The Chicago All Stars were typical jump blues combos…consisted of band leaders…who could also sing… Sugarman Penigar… Johnny Motion and Cozy Eggleston shared the vocals" (RST Records, 1994).

My parents sang vocals during their performances on stage during their gigs. My mother sang this song called "Love for Sale" written by Cole Porter in 1930. My mom would flirt with my dad as she sang the song. It was electrifying to watch. Wonderful acting on their parts too. Tony Bennett and Lady Gaga did a version of the song released on September 17, 2021.

12	Chicago Allstars* –	Are You Getting Married, Brother?	3:11

Alto Saxophone, Clarinet – Oett "Sax" Mallard
Contrabass [Stringbass] – Bali Beach
Drums – Armand "Jump" Jackson
Guitar – Elmer Ewing
Piano – Bill Owens (10)
Tenor Saxophone – Edgar "Sugarman" Penigar*
Trumpet – Johnny Morton
Vocals – Cozy Eggleston

19

My Parents Later in Life

Contrary to my parents' interest in music, neither my brother nor sister or I had an interest in playing a musical instrument. They played musical instruments; however, we had no desire, which was somewhat rare in families. Both parents were musicians and had careers in the field of music. Our parents didn't push it on us either. I didn't want to play an instrument, nor did my siblings. But we really loved music, singing, and dancing. I remember how difficult it was for my parents to find gigs after returning to Chicago from traveling. However, when they did find a gig, they'd make more money from one gig than others made from a month's work. Though, that factor didn't matter to me at all. I recall saying to myself that I wanted more financial security in life with a stable job. I wanted a guaranteed weekly or monthly check for my work efforts.

My dad began talking about some of his and my mom's recent activities. Although they still played music, they slowed down a bit from doing gigs. They embarked upon other opportunities. Filmmakers loved making movies in Chicago. So whenever that came, my parents would show up for auditions. They never got speaking roles, but film producers selected them to be in movie scenes. For instance, my mother was in the movie *The Fugitive*. She was in the scene when Harrison Ford, the actor, was fighting with the one-armed man. She's sitting on the subway train as shown in the picture.

My mom told me that Harrison Ford liked her so much that he wanted her to have a speaking role while on the train. He wanted to turn and ask her if she was okay. However, it didn't make sense since he had to focus on fighting the one-armed man. He did let her sit in his chair when they were on set. My mom did have a very charming and sweet personality.

She was in an all-girl band too. On many occasions, they would play gigs in Chicago.

My father was in the movie *Blue Chip* with Nick Nolte, written by Ron Shelton and released in 1994. It is about a college coach trying to improve his basketball team with new recruits. My father was in the scene when Nick Nolte came to Chicago to recruit a basketball player. The player lived in the projects, as they were called. My father was standing by the door as Nick Nolte entered. My dad had me cracking up when he told me he said, "Hey, brother Nolte," as Nolte walked into the building. I asked him what made him say that as they were filming. Nolte wasn't playing himself in the movie. He was a character. My dad explained he didn't know what made him say that. Anyway, they deleted the sound bite but kept the scene. The movie producers liked the hat my dad wore during the audition. My dad was well known throughout Chicago for the different types of brims he wore. He had a hat for every outfit he wore. Those hats became his brand. Everyone recognized him as soon as they saw him wearing his hats.

My dad in a white cap and in the scene with
Nick Nolte entering the building

Not only did filmmakers use my parents in movie scenes but they also used their music in movie soundtracks. His music is part of a soundtrack for the movie *Going All the Way*, with Ben Affleck, in 1998. Dad began to discuss the setting for the movie and said, "There were two soldiers returning home to Indianapolis. These two guys had just gotten out of the army. They went back to their home in Indianapolis and were making it out to all the joints and everything. I went to see this movie since I knew my music was in it. They called me from Los Angeles to tell me that they wanted to use my music in this movie." He went on to describe the scene and said, "Ben Affleck and his buddy went into a club one night. Ben Affleck told his buddy to put something in the jukebox so they could hear some music. So his buddy went and put some money in the jukebox." Then my Dad said to me, "You could hear the money falling down in the jukebox. You know how you can hear money drop down into the jukebox? That's when my tune came up. They played my tune 'Big Heavy.' They had known each other before they went into the army. When they were returning home from the army, they remembered each other."

Again, I googled about his music being in the movie and found it to be true.

Going All the Way (1997)

Soundtracks (20)

A White Sport Coat And A Pink Carnation
Written and Performed by Marty Robbins
Courtesy of Columbia Records
by arrangement with Sony Music Licensing

Fast Blues
Written and Performed by Jimmy Coe
Courtesy of Delmark Records

Poodgy
Written and Performed by Bobby Smith
Courtesy of Delmark Records

Big Heavy
Written and Performed by Cozy Eggleston
Courtesy of Delmark Records

Later in my parents' career, they didn't play as many gigs as they did early in their career. My dad still played a few gigs every now and then. They didn't have to provide direct care for us as we had gone off to college. When I was home from college on spring break, I remember club-hopping with my brother and other college classmates. We went to one club, and the man carding the people at the door saw my ID. He noticed I wasn't old enough to enter. At the time, driver's licenses weren't laminated. I stepped out of line. I took a pen out of my purse and pushed my age up by a year so I could enter. Well, the man noticed I had changed the date of birth on my ID and told me so. I couldn't pull the wool over his eyes, as the saying goes. My brother and our friends did not like partying with me in my freshman year as I was seventeen, not eighteen yet. So we ended up going to a club where my dad was playing. When we arrived, we told the man who was at the door that our dad and his band were playing there. He let us enter. As we were going to one of the vacant tables to be seated, my dad was on intermission and came over to greet us. He told the bartender not to give me any alcoholic beverage because I wasn't of age. I was kind of embarrassed. However, in the back of my mind, knowing my dad, I thought it was kind of special. Because it was a jazz club with older patrons, it was out of touch with what we wanted to do. So we didn't stay long. We wanted to dance and party with our peers. We stayed awhile and left.

The musicians' union would get opportunities for them to perform in larger venues. One such venue was the ChicagoFest jazz festival, held annually in the summer at Navy Pier. There were sixteen stages, with each highlighting the various forms of music including jazz. I attended the ChicagoFest in 1981 to watch my parents play right before I relocated to Oklahoma.

My father played in other jazz festivals in Chicago too. The Chicago Park District held a jazz summer in the Park Jazz Festivals. My father has been in commercials, "Chicago Blues", playing his sax. In 2001, he played his sax in another commercial advertising for Singapore Airlines. My father allowed a man from overseas to use his music. He received royalties. My siblings and I continue to receive royalties from our parent's music.

20

The Last Chapter

Watching my mom and dad as musicians and having them as parents was truly a blessing. Moving through my life stages and remembering everything they taught me was so beneficial. My father always taught us to never let anyone or anything get in the way of our hopes, dreams, and goals. Later in my life, I wanted to learn how to play the saxophone. Right before going away to college for my freshman year, my mother started teaching me. She was teaching me how to play the musical scale on her alto sax. However, I didn't have the time to travel back and forth between Champaign and Chicago, so the lessons stopped. I had to focus on my studies.

By going away to college and moving to Oklahoma, I wasn't able to be around them much. We kept in contact often. They wouldn't miss sending me cards for my birthday. They would always eat healthily. They even had a garden on the lot they purchased next to our home in Bronzeville, on Giles Avenue. They grew tomatoes, green beans, and an array of other vegetables. My mom would cook them for me whenever I'd visit. She even had a plant in our backyard that produced sweet, edible large red strawberries.

Yes, my father was a musician; however, there are many things about him people don't know. He was a carpenter who completely rebuilt the porch and the steps leading to the backyard of our house. He told me he learned carpentry while in the CC camp.

Another one of his favorite passions was playing checkers. It was a hobby he loved playing with the men in the neighborhood. They'd always gather in the neighborhood to play. He loved it so much that he made his own large checkerboard out of plywood. He drew the squares on top and painted each one. He was really good. He often beat every opponent. We often played because I wanted him to teach me how to play. I thought that since he was my father, he would let me win. However, that wasn't the case; I was on my own and lost to him often. My father is the man with the beard and sideburns on the left in the picture. He's playing checkers on the board he made, contemplating his next move.

During my childhood, my father loved to hunt. Although he was a city-bred man and a leader of a jazz band, he was an avid huntsman. My father tried to foster my brother James's interest in hunting. He took James with him on a hunting trip. Well, when they came across an animal, my brother held his rifle with a tight grip. My dad was standing there in anticipation of the big moment; however, my brother could not pull the trigger. He didn't want to kill any animals. That was the end of my brother's hunting experience. Hunting was not for him! My dad had a hunting dog named Skeater. He was also the family dog. Skeater thought he was a human. He would sit up in the front seat of our car. People thought he was a human sitting there. Our whole neighborhood loved him. I loved Skeater. He was the neighborhood dog too. My dad would take Skeater with him to hunt for fun and put food on the table. I remember him hunting rabbit, squirrel, deer, possum, pheasant, deer, and raccoon. My mother was an avid cook. She used recipes from the *Betty Crocker Cookbook*. She made savory dishes for us using the meat my dad captured while hunting. The pheasant under glass, the rabbit cacciatore, and the baked raccoon with sweet potatoes were all wonderful tasty delicacies. However, I didn't care much for the possum. My dad came home very early one morning after hunting and woke me up out of my sleep, holding a raccoon in my face. It frightened me so much it's probably why I didn't want to eat any of it.

My mother knew how to make canned goods. Canning is the process of preserving food in jars to last for a long time. I don't know where she picked up the skill, but she was very good at it. She could can just about all kinds of food. She made jelly and preserves from fresh fruit. She canned fresh fruit and vegetables. She made cha cha, which is a relish made with green tomatoes, onions, cabbage, and peppers. It can be made either sweet or hot.

My parents would take us to the "country," or outskirts of Chicago, to purchase bushels of pears and peaches to can. My siblings and I were the ones who peeled and cut up the fruit for canning. This was a very tedious job. We kind of hated it with a passion. We had a station wagon at the time, which is an old version of the current SUV. So on the way home, we started taking the fruit from the back of the car. We started throwing it out of the window into the street in our neighborhood close to our house. The more fruit we threw out of the window, the less we had to peel.

Right after returning home from getting the fruit, we had to go to the store. The fruit was still in the car in bushel baskets. Well, little did we know that my parents drove down the same street where we'd thrown the fruit. We were terrified as we got close to the crime scene. We thought, *Why did they have to drive that route to the store?* My parents noticed the pears and asked, "How did all of this fruit get in the streets?" We looked at one another and told them that we didn't know. They let it slide. We were so happy they didn't dig deeper. In the back of their minds, I bet they knew it was us. Who else could've done it? My siblings and I spent much of our school's spring break time peeling and coring fruit for canning. Now I wish I would have learned my mom's canning skills. In addition, they had us complete household chores during our school's cleanup week. We washed walls; painted, dusted, and waxed furniture; and mopped and waxed floors. They were teaching us how to be responsible. We couldn't wait to get back to school.

My father wanted us to be proficient in all of our class subjects in school, especially math. He believed that being adept in math was the key to every aspect of success in life. We did many things together as a family. So, to help us in math, he purchased a Monopoly game. He wanted us to have a strong business sense. We bought and sold property while playing the game. I was very frugal with my money. However, my brother would buy up every piece of property where his token landed. He'd purchase and buy houses for the expensive boardwalk property. He bought up everything and would end up going bankrupt. It's so ironic my brother ended up in a lucrative side business in real estate. Anyway, my dad felt the game Monopoly would teach us how to count money too. Whenever he'd send us to the store to buy something, he'd give us a twenty-dollar bill. If the item cost $12.52, we'd have to count the change in chronological order to reach $20.

While in grammar school, my class was learning multiplication-table integers one–twelve. My father knew it too. So when I returned home from school, he'd meet me at the front door. As soon as I walked into the house, he'd ask me to recite the multiplication table. We stood in the entry each time, no sitting. We both stood as I recited. The ones were easy. I knew the twos because we called them out while jumping rope called double Dutch. When I got to the larger numbers—the eights and the nines—the trouble began. He was a tall man in stature, big and strong. As I walked home, I dreaded it because I knew he'd be there, waiting for me. It was time to recite the eights. He watched me with each breath. I stood there, reciting each integer. My voice was cracking as I started. Shaking in my boots, I recited—"Eight times eight is sixty-four. Eight times nine is seventy-two…"—to the end. I felt that the days I spent learning and reciting the multiplication table for my dad were the worst days of my life. Little did I know how much my father's persistence in knowing math would help later in life. In my first job interview after college graduation, the interviewer gave me a task. She gave me a program budget to review. I found errors in the math calculations and pointed them out to the interviewer. I secured the position with the company. During a staff meeting with board members present, the director introduced me. He said, "And she's not afraid of numbers either." All accolades go to my father. When he met me at the door at home to recite my tables, I was petrified. In retrospect, that was one of many encounters contributing to my success in life.

I remember being home one day when I was in eighth grade. One of the animals Skeater was hunting got a hold of him and deeply scratched him on his side. I let him in my bed and was comforting him. My dad called his veterinarian to help with the swollen wound. He told my dad to place a solution of warm salt and water, heavy on the salt, onto the wound. Dad followed the veterinarian's instructions. As I watched, I saw the drainage oozing from the wound. I couldn't believe my eyes. That salt-and-water solution drew all the pus from the cut out of the dog's wound. Skeater healed quickly after that. I guess that's why the older generation, including my parents, had my siblings and me gargle with warm salt water. It truly soothed our throats. It really worked.

Our next-door neighbor was a mean and wicked old lady. She'd paint her chain-link fence black and spread heavy grease all over it while it was still wet. She did it to keep us from leaning on it. She had a dog that died. While I was away in college, I would ask about Skeater. When I arrived home on break, I ran into the house to see Skeater. I didn't see him, and that was when my parents told me Skeater had passed. They didn't want to tell me when I asked before coming home for a break. They waited. They remembered how I had cried my heart out when our parakeet, Pete, passed away. Pete passed the Christmas before I went away to college. It was Christmas Eve when we found

Pete lying still on the bottom of his cage. We'd taught him a few tricks and how to tweet out his name. I was so heart-broken for the bird. I was crying for a bird like I'd lost a family member or something. Well, my parents told me the mean old lady who lived next door was so upset her dog had passed. We assume her jealousy of our dog being alive while her dog had passed drove her to poison Skeater. She had thrown the poison over the back fence. Anyway, the mean next-door neighbor had a heart attack alone in her house. She was found dead in her home, clutching her phone. As people say, God does not like ugly. From that point on, during my college school breaks, being back home, I surely did miss Skeater.

When our family moved back to Chicago in 1956, my mother didn't play in as many gigs as my dad. She did play in some but mainly stayed home to care for us. My mom played her alto saxophone, but she was good at a lot of other things. I already mentioned her cooking skills, but she also had a green thumb. She grew all kinds of house-plants and had a beautiful large flower bed in front of the lot next to our house. My parents purchased two lots to the right of our house. We used the one next to the house as an extension of our backyard. We held family cookouts and Easter egg hunts there. I held my African wedding cer-emony in that lot too. The lot next to it was where my par-ents planted their vegetable garden. My parents gave their neighbors access to the garden at no charge.

Well, when we became a bit older, my mother took a test to work at the post office. She passed with flying colors to become the first female letter carrier at the Lincoln Park post office. Her job was an easy one. She delivered mail to residents who resided on the Gold Coast—an affluent area in Chicago's North Side. Residents lived in lavish multi-story buildings. She didn't have a door-to-door route and only delivered to a few buildings there. When she retired, the *Chicago* magazine did a story about her. Here are a few excerpts from the article:

> Marie Eggleston pushed her mail cart along her Lincoln Park route, radio headphones clamped firmly over her ears. I asked what was she listening to. "Canned music," she responded with an uncharacteristic touch of grumpiness. "The kind that puts me out of work." Eggleston has been a letter carrier for 20 years and a jazz saxophonist for close to 50. She's played at clubs from New York to North Dakota, St Louis to Canada…old Chicago clubs…entertained at Daley Plaza and at Chicago Fest…led by her husband, Cozy Eggleston, or fronting her own, Marie Stone and All Girls. In her first professional job she played the blues at the Cue Lounge at 35th and State…in 1938 and Marie was 18 years old. (Kiefer 1885, 130)

After my mom retired, my parents attended the Urban League for a computer class. She would send me email messages from their computer. She picked it up quickly. She would help my dad during class. Once, they told me the instructor separated them in the classroom. The instructor wanted my dad to learn on his own without my mom's help. It took a long time for my dad to send me a message. Finally, he typed one for me on their home computer. I was so elated when he did.

While living in Champaign, Illinois, after obtaining my first degree, I got my dad a gig at one of the nightclubs there. He loved sponge cake and sherbet. During intermissions, I honored him with some. I told the audience that we should honor people while they're alive and not when they're gone. When my parents turned seventy, I started giving them a dollar for every year they lived. I guess I was using the money to encourage them to live to get those dollars.

My sister, Ms. Brick House, and I, Disco Slim, performing on stage

Left to right; me, my sister Rosemarie Eggleston,
and my brother James Eggleston
Name of group: The Affair

117

As mentioned earlier, my siblings and I had no interest in playing a musical instrument. However, we loved singing and dancing. While living in Champaign, Illinois, my sister and brother formed a group in Chicago called the Affair. After moving back to Chicago in 1979 from Champaign-Urbana, Illinois, I joined the group. Our father, as our manager, obtained gigs for us in Chicago and surrounding areas including Gary, Indiana. I saw the joy on my dad's face while we performed on stage. He was definitely in his element, being a leader of his own band for most of his life. He was most proud because we were his offspring. We weren't musicians playing instruments, but we were a part of the music industry as entertainers.

Because of my dance background in choreography, performance, and production, I called myself Disco Slim. I performed a dance routine during our gigs to the song "Bad Girls" by Donna Summer. In addition, I danced to conga drums played by my brother and another member of our group. While in college in Champaign, my brother had taken classes to learn how to play conga drums. A master drummer from Ghana, Amoaku, taught the class.

My sister, with her dynamic body shape, called herself Ms. Brick House, and it was very fitting. My sister and I coordinated our outfits to wear on stage. We learned from a wonderful mentor: our mother, who we watched as she prepared for the stage. We dressed in style. We performed songs that were popular during the time of our group's existence. Of course, we sang "Bad Girls" by Donna Summer, "Ladies Night" by Kool & the Gang, "Give It to Me Baby" by Rick James, "Good Times" by Chic, "Brick House" by the Commodores, and "Heartbreak Hotel" by the Jacksons, just to name a few. I sang solo "You Know How to Love Me" by Phyllis Hyman. I held that long note too. Our group, the Affair, ended its stint right before I moved to Oklahoma in 1981. Those were the good old days, as people say. I will cherish those days forever.

Whenever I took a vacation from work in Oklahoma, I would always go home to Chicago to see my parents. There were no trips for me to the Bahamas or elsewhere; I wanted to spend time with my parents. I would stay at our house with them too. Although I was an adult, my dad and I would go pick out a fresh pine tree for Christmas. I loved the smell of the tree, with the aroma going throughout the house. We used the same items when I was a little girl living at home to decorate the tree. Seeing those items stirred up warm memories. I had my favorite decorative pieces too. My dad still directed me to where to place the items on the tree. He loved it with a passion. I guess that was part of his makeup, being a band leader and all. When my siblings and I were younger, it would really get on our nerves. After my parents went to bed, my siblings and I would take the items and place them where we wanted. We took pride in our Christmas tree. We placed it by the large window in the front room, facing the street. We would all venture outside to see how it looked. It was a glorious sight to see with the lights placed around the windows. Picking out a fresh tree and decorating it became a long-standing family tradition. I continued to visit my parents over the years.

One Christmas, while visiting my parents, my mom looked awfully skinny. She was never a thin woman in her adult life. So I attributed her change in weight to being part of aging. My mother was not gaining weight either. My dad, being concerned, took her to the doctor. That's when we got the bad news of my mother's diagnosis: pancreatic cancer. Her prognosis was four to six months to live. I was totally devastated. This occurred in January right after my visit for Christmas when I noticed my mom's weight loss.

My daughter was in rotations at the time, which is during the last year two years of medical school. During rotations, medical students shadow doctors in various clinical settings. My mom was so proud of my daughter. She told the hospital staff that her granddaughter was a doctor. My daughter would meet my mom's doctors during their rounds to discuss my mom's health status. She told me my mom was so happy to see her. My daughter became the point of contact for our family for information on my mom's health. Actually, it was my daughter who gave us my mother's horrid prognosis of four to six months to live.

It was during the month of her birthday—March—in 2002. I visited my parents in Chicago. I came to be there for her birthday. My son picked me up from the airport. I was so elated about my daughter completing her coursework. She was going to graduate in May, which was a couple of months away. My son and I were talking about getting the graduation invites ready and who to invite. The school was giving only a limited number of invites to attendees. I remember telling my son enthusiastically how my mother was going to be at the graduation. I will never forget the look he had on his face when he turned to me and said, "Grandma isn't going to be able to go to the graduation." Since he lived in Chicago and I didn't, he knew more about the frailty of my mom's health. After my son told me that, I gazed away, staring into space, bewildered. That was something I did not want to face. We made it to my parents' house. I rushed in, and it was then I understood what my son meant.

Once I got settled, I gave my mom her gift. I continued my ritual of giving one dollar to represent each year of her life. I counted out $84 as I placed it in her hands for her eighty-fourth birthday on March 6, 2002. She wanted to go to Sears, where my parents had an account for many years. She had told me of her delight in watching the selling of jewelry on the QVC television channel. So my dad drove us to Sears so she could buy jewelry with her birthday money. She was walking at a very slow pace through the store. I slowed my pace to stay by her. It was then I realized my mother was not in good health. It hit me hard that she was in her final stage of life. My time with her was fading. She picked out and purchased a beautiful ring with the $84 I gave her for her birthday.

My dad purchased my mom a cell phone too. She was very tech savvy and knew how to use it. I told her to call me after I returned to my house in Oklahoma. Before returning to Oklahoma, I purchased two cameras with microphones so we could Skype each other—one for her and one for me. With Skype, we could see and talk to each other. We Skyped each other several times. There was no FaceTime then.

My mom started treatments for her medical condition. I took time off work again to go to Chicago to take her to her treatments. Those treatments drained her, but I told her she was doing good and to stay strong. My mother didn't quite make the four to six months given her by the physicians. It was two months and nineteen days after her eighty-fourth birthday on March 6, 2002. She passed away about four months after the diagnosis, on May 25, 2002. This was one of the most devastating losses I've had since the passing of my grandparents. Not only was it traumatic for me, but more so for my father. My parents had known each other for close to fifty-six years.

In May 2002, I traveled to Chicago. I had to attend two events. One was my daughter's graduation from medical school, and the other was my mom's funeral. I was numb. On one hand, I was proud of my daughter graduating. On the other, I was sad to see my mom go. I was walking around in a daze. It was a bittersweet moment in my life.

Usually, it's a phenomenon; when one spouse passes, the other one goes right after. I thought about it after my mom passed. So I spent as much time with my father as I could. I still lived in Oklahoma and constantly called him right after my mom passed. Once, I called, and there was no answer. I kept calling over and over. I panicked and called my sister, who lived near him. I couldn't get through to her. So I called my best friend, who lived up the street from him. She told me she had just seen him standing on the front porch. I was relieved. On another occasion, while talking to him on the phone, I said something to him. He didn't say anything back to me. I called back, and the phone was busy. He called me back and said he'd fallen asleep while talking to me. Such stress. After my mom passed, my brother, my sister, and I kept in close contact with our father. Since my siblings lived in Chicago, they were able to go check on him. I couldn't because I lived in Oklahoma.

My father exhibited strength, maintaining himself after Mom passed. He had a good support system. He continued to eat healthily. He was exercising. He told me earlier in life about the calisthenics he did while in the army. He demonstrated them to me at that time. He kept doing them. Both parents rode their bicycles around the neighborhood. They purchased a stationary bike to cycle indoors at home. My dad continued to use the stationary bike in his house. Also, my father kept himself active in his music. He continued to live alone in our two-story home. I traveled to Chicago to watch him play in his annual Summer Concert in the Park gig. It was such a fun time. It felt strange to see my father play in a gig without my mother. It was another bittersweet moment. Dad and his band played at the Sixty-Third Street Beach location for the Concerts in the Park event.

This pic is one of a park gig where my parents played
together in their band in 2001. My parents are sitting next
to each other, blowing their sax on the left in picture.

During one visit to Chicago to see my dad, he had to
get his cataracts removed. He loved going to the Veterans
hospital to see his doctors. He was one man of few who
believed in preventative care. It was an outing for him too.
He dressed up, wearing his trendy hats. I had to drive him

home after his cataract surgery. He was so used to being in control, driving his car. He had a domineering personality. He was a strong patriarch of our family. Also, being a band leader played a part. He was a good leader, holding things together at work and at home. He stayed by his family and never abandoned us. I will always cherish his character for that. Anyway, during our drive home, he started telling me how to drive, which way to go, and how fast to go. But I was in control. He was getting so upset with me because I wasn't doing what he was telling me. Intentionally I sped up very fast. I was really getting on his last nerve. He couldn't take it, so he started fussing and grabbing at the steering wheel. I told him that he was going to cause an accident. He settled down, and we made it home safely. That was the funniest thing. I remember it like it was just yesterday.

My father continued to drive. To go downtown, he'd park his car on a side street close to the aboveground subway. He lived closer to downtown, which was about twenty minutes from our house by subway. It's called the "L" train in Chicago, with some routes aboveground and belowground. It travels underground upon reaching the downtown area. The aboveground section was close to our house. One time, he parked his car and walked to the train to go downtown. However, while returning home, he went to the location and couldn't locate his car. He informed my siblings. They accompanied him to find his car. Traffic was heavy at the time, and there were many parked cars on the street. They didn't find it. They were going to report the car as stolen. About a couple of days later, they saw his car sitting in the spot where he'd parked it. Later, he'd had a couple of minor car accidents. My father was so independent. Older adults feel they lose a major part of their independence when they give up driving. However, my siblings and I knew it was time to have that dreaded "talk" with our father. It was time for him to give up his car keys.

During that time, he very seldom played his tenor saxophone. He didn't play any gigs at all. However, people were still interested in his music. I remember one visit where he wanted me to go with him to downtown Chicago. Some guys wanted to purchase some of his albums. I went with him. We met the buyers at their place of business. I couldn't believe how much money they paid for those albums. Dad walked away with over $450 for about three albums he sold. They paid approximately $150 per album.

My father continued to live home alone in our two-story home. My siblings informed me that our father had difficulty climbing the steep stairs to go to the second story. You know how people would cover the carpet with plastic to minimize wear and tear? Well, that plastic was on the steps of the staircase. As dad walked up the stairs, the plastic would slip underneath his feet. This was a disaster waiting to happen. Going to the VA hospital with Dad, I developed a rapport with his doctor. So I called his doctor to get a referral to get a lift. He gave approval. I called a medical equipment company and arranged its installation. I wasn't in Chicago to oversee it. I called my dad later that week, and the company had installed the lift. I felt so much better for safety purposes. My brother purchased a monitoring device. You place it around your neck and press it if you fall or need assistance. They removed the plastic runner also.

As time continued, my father's health started to decline. The older one gets, the more likely some health issues will crop up. My siblings secured a home health aide to assist with meals and light housekeeping. As Dad's health continued to decline, my brother became his primary caregiver. He called me to come to Chicago because he needed relief. We tried to keep it up, but to no avail. At first, we placed him in an assisted living facility. However, he needed more direct care. Eventually, we had to place him in a nursing facility. He thrived for some time. I'd visit him there and take videos of him talking. He started having to go back and forth to the hospital because of health issues. He was in the hospital when I went to visit my daughter in another state. I needed a reprieve from the situation. My sister called and told me Dad wasn't talking at all. She told me that since I was his favorite, I must return to see him. I drove nonstop for twelve hours to Chicago. I drove directly to the hospital. I entered my dad's room, and there he was, lying in bed. When I approached him, he turned to me and said, "Where have you been?" My sister was so happy he talked. Well, thereafter, within that week, my sister called to tell me to come to the hospital. I got there, ready to see my dad. All my siblings were there and my nephews too. That's when they told me our father had passed. Those words were so gut-wrenching to my very soul. I went to his room to see him. He looked at peace. Both of my parents were gone. He passed on December 7, 2012, which was ten years after my mom. He hung in there to the age of ninety-two. I was blessed to have had him in my life that long.

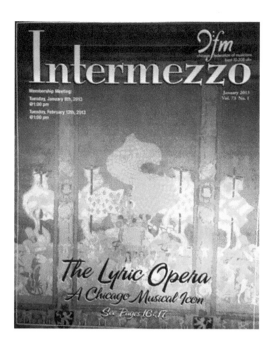

I'd written in my career. So I wrote my dad's obituary. That was the most difficult writing I'd ever done. I contacted the local musicians' union (10-208) to obtain funds on behalf of my father. They set up funds for their members to help cover the cost of burial expenses. Throughout the years, my parents would always be active with the Local 10-208 musicians' union. On several occasions, I went with my father when he visited there. He loved going there. Everyone knew him and my mom because they had been members for a long time. My parents loved to dress up—"get sharp," as they called it—to attend the annual Musicians' Union Banquet. They never missed attending the banquet. It was always a big highlight for them. When I visited the union, I told them of my father's passing. They approved the financial assistance and made it readily available. Before I left, they gave me a bunch of pictures they had of my parents from over the years. They truly admired and respected them. They'd been union members throughout the duration of their career. Dad was a member for sixty-seven years. Since he was a veteran with an honorable discharge, he's buried at the Veteran's cemetery. It was a beautiful ceremony with a gun salute and the folding of the American flag. My father would always say while toasting champagne, "May I live forever and never die." No one lives forever, but he put up a darn good fight. My siblings and I were blessed to have had our father in our lives for that long.

The Local 10-208 musicians' union publishes a magazine called the *Intermezzo*. They wrote an article about him after he passed.

Here are excerpts from the article:

> He attended the Chicago Conservatory School of Music. He was a Tenor saxophonist. He worked with big bands early in his career. He returned home to Chicago and formed his own band…his wife, calling herself Marie Stone, was a member. "Cozy" was his stage name. He traveled throughout the United States and overseas with his band. He and his band were well known in Europe. He loved his music. He acquired Co-Egg and Production company to publish his music. Big Heavy was used as the theme song by

Hound Dog on radio station WBKW in Buffalo, New York. He appeared at the Chicago Jazz Festival for several years... Cozy also played at the Chicago Park District's Summer Jazz Series for many years through the Musician's union. In 2005, he was honored by the Hyde Park Jazz Society.

Over the years since my parents passed, I've come across many articles about them. I came across some of the articles while completing research for this book. Some of the information was new to me because I wasn't even born yet. It was so fulfilling to see my parents get recognition for their musical accomplishments.

I came upon one such article from the blog *Russ & Gary's "The Best Years of Music."* It's from their daily archives, specifically the one on November 10, 2010, titled "Russ's Old 78s—R&B Album" (strathdee.wordpress.com). The article highlights twelve artists. My dad is one of them. Here are excerpts from the article:

> "Tenor sax player C.J. "Cozy" Eggleston (born May 12, 1920) emerged during the flourishing Chicago postwar scene. An early gig (October 1946 through January 1947) was at the Macomb Lounge (39th and Cottage Grove)... In 1956 he recorded for Columbia with a group called the Memphis Seven. For a time he played in

Lil Green's band, and used a pianist named Sony Blount (who had likewise been in the Green band) in his own combo. In 1949, he appeared at the Manchester Green his wife Marie Stone Eggleston… ace musician, and the bombshell of the alto sax… Marie, who changed her name to Marie Stone to tour with Cozy… Back in those days, people frowned on married couples working in the same band… By the time of his States recording session on August 23, 1952, Eggleston had one hot and popular band… Cozy himself played the smoking sax… "Big Heavy"… The year 1955 saw this recording used further as a radio show theme tune by George "Hound Dog" Lorenz's each weeknight… over WKBW in Buffalo, NY serving the entire Eastern seaboard.

Other artists highlighted in the article include Amos Milburn, Big Connie, the Crawford Brothers, Freddie Strong, Guitar Gable, Little Junior's Blue Flames, Lloyd Lambert, Shirley & Lee, Sonny Thompson, and Wynonie Harris.

Once, while on a social media platform, I saw an article about my parents. There was contact information for the author. His name is Jeff Ash. I texted him, letting him know the article was about my parents. He told me he was writing an article on a totally different subject. He indicated that while going through newspaper archives, he saw something that caught his eye. He happened upon many articles about my parents and decided to write a story about them. He resides in Green Bay, Wisconsin. After reading the article, the content jogged my memory. I remember when they played there and the names of the places. We were older then when they left to work in Green Bay. They became fans of the Green Bay Packers. Often, they'd tell us about the friends they met who would always come to see them perform. The author of the article and I still keep in touch to this very day. Here are excerpts from the article "Getting Cozy at the Club" in the *AM, Then FM* blog:

> Chicago sax man Cozy Eggleston and his swinging jazz combo played a four-night gig as the Club Coal Bin in Green Bay had its grand opening. The club was in the basement of the Labor Temple. It's slogan, U.S.G.S.T.,stood for "Us Swingers Gotta Stick Together." The club apparently was trying to class up its act. It used to be…a strip joint… Even though Cozy Eggleston had become the main attraction, it was unnatural to see black performers at Green Bay nightclubs, even in 1968… March 1968, when Cozy and his combo played the club in the basement of the Labor Temple… They were brought back two weeks later for a return engagement said to be "by popular demand." Cozy produced and

released… "Grand Slam" on their Co-Egg label… DownBeat columnist John…calls this record an "an all-out soul blue flame" and a "classic." It features, Cozy, Marie, Karl Johnson on the Hammond organ and Ken Sampson on drums… Cozy produced and released "Whammin & Slammin"… Chicago Tribune reviewer John Litweiler called it "straight-ahead organ-sax band entertainment" from Cozy, whom they called "one of Gene Ammons' many musical offspring"… Cozy Eggleston, who was 48 when he played that basement club in Green Bay in March 1968, kept playing for years. (Ash 2018)

Jeff Ash sent a multitude of information on my parents. Here are excerpts from a newspaper article from a Green Bay newspaper:

Saxophonist Cozy Eggleston is at the Coal Bin… Cozy said jazz is his bag because "there's never an end to what you can do. You could play a song for 40 years and never stop learning. You keep fishing around and always learn"… Cozy is an example of utmost "I can take a tune and sax song it… I can hear it once and play it… Foreign audiences are more responsive than those in the states"… Cozy has his favorite from the past too "Lester Young was my idol. I wanted to play like him because he was from the cool school. Does he copy the style of Lester Young? "No, I'm thinking for myself. When I first started off, I sounded like him. But not anymore. I still play some of his things, but I play them in my own way. I've got my own way." He sings too. Are there any sax players today that are 20 years ahead of their time? "No, I don't think so. There's not too many geniuses born...there's only so many things you can play." With Cozy are Karl Johnson, organ; Eddie Chappell, drums; and Raina Taylor, vocals. The Chicago Quartet is from Chicago. (Gerds 1969)

Jeff Ash completed research and found a historical compilation of articles about my parents. He sent information in an email to me on May 5, 2022, as follows:

Jeff Ash says all of the following are from the Green Bay Press-Gazette:
"Dancing and Entertainment" ad from April 27, 1951.
"Greatest Entertainment Value" ad from Jan. 9, 1953.

Club Coal Bin grand opening ad from March 5, 1968 (U.S.G.S.T. stands for Us Swingers Gotta Stick Together)

Interview "Jazz Is the Thing They Do the Best" from Aug. 8, 1969.

Brief story "Has a Hit" from May 4, 1972.

"Opening Tonight in the Atrium Room" ad from Oct. 18, 1971.

Interview "First Impressions Can Be Deceiving" from Oct. 21, 1971.

This clip is from the Sheboygan Press: Tic Toc Tap ad from Oct. 1, 1956.

Now some other notes of possible interest from old newspapers (and this all I'll have for you)...

The first time Cozy Eggleston shows up in the old papers is in the Detroit Free Press on Feb. 9, 1946. (It's attached.) He's playing at the Paradise Theatre in Detroit. That was in the Paradise Valley section of Detroit, the city's Black business and entertainment center. The surrounding Black residential area was called Black Bottom.

Some info about that area...

http://www.blackbottomarchives.com/blackhistory/2016/2/16/remembering-paradise-valley

https://detroithistorical.org/learn/
encyclopedia-of-detroit/paradise-valley

The next time Cozy appears in the old papers is that 1951 ad from Green Bay I sent the other night. They really must have loved him in Green Bay, because he turns up more in the old Green Bay Press-Gazette issues than any newspaper besides the Chicago Tribune.

Here's a timeline of gigs mentioned in the old papers available to be searched online. I'm sure it's far from complete. Not sure on a couple of them.

February 1946—Paradise Theatre in Detroit.

April 1951—The Piccadilly in Green Bay.

July 1951 and August 1952—Basil's in Kokomo, Indiana.

October 1951—The Terrace Lounge in East St. Louis, Illinois.

April and May 1952—Club Zanzibar in Sandusky, Ohio

July 1952—the Decatur Cocktail Lounge in Decatur, Illinois.

December 1952 and January 1953—The Piccadilly in Green Bay.

May 1953—Club Normandy in Mishawaka, Indiana.

July 1953—The Tropics in Sioux Falls, South Dakota.

April 1954—The Piccadilly in Green Bay.

December 1954—The New Kentucky Lounge at 6725 S. Ashland Ave. in Chicago (Englewood).

Late 1955 or early 1956—The Playdium Lounge in East St. Louis, Illinois.

July 1956—Club DeVille, 2600 S. State St. in Chicago?

October 1956—The Tic Toc Tap in Sheboygan, Wisconsin.

May 1957—The Piccadilly in Green Bay.

January 1961—Mickey's Lounge at 5639 W. Roosevelt Road in Cicero. (Ad for this, from January 14, 1961, is attached.)

March 1961—Frank's Steak House in Streator, Illinois

February 1962—The Dude Ranch at 8039 Ogden Ave. in Lyons.

June 1962—Paul and Gene's Club Grove in Streator, Illinois (same place as in 1961)

October 1962—The Pad on North State Street in Chicago?

December 1964—Jimmy Purcell's Femme 'A Go-Go at 3196 Milwaukee

Ave. in Chicago. (Building is still there, at Belmont.)

March, April, May and June 1968— Club Coal Bin in Green Bay.

Tuesday, June 24, 1969—Cozy plays in a benefit jam session with some big names, and hosted by Merri Dee of WBEE radio, at The Living Room at 744 E. 83rd St. in Chicago. (I've attached that clipping from the Chicago Tribune of June 27, 1969. That building also appears to still be there.)

August 1969—Club Coal Bin in Green Bay.

February 1971—the Sabre Lounge at 5611 W. Grand Ave. in Chicago.

October 1971—Bilotti's Forum in Green Bay.

From 1981 to 2007, there are 30 or so listings in the Chicago Tribune of local shows Cozy played—Chicagofest jazz stage, Green Mill Jazz Club, Pops for Champagne, Chicago Jazz Festival, West Pullman Park, Rosenblum Park and 63rd Street Beach.

Hope this fills in some of the gaps. Wish you all the success with your project. Be well! Thanks, Jeff Ash, Green Bay.

The pics sent from Jeff Ash's research efforts are as follows:

My parents are in the center of this picture

One day, while checking my Messenger account, I saw correspondence from someone I didn't know. The message was from Steven Krakow, and he wrote, "Is this the daughter of Cozy? I'd like to do an article on him for the *Chicago Reader*." I told him that yes, he's my father. Krakow writes articles for the *Chicago Reader*. It is an alternative weekly newspaper in Chicago, Illinois, founded on October 1, 1971. "Steven Krakow, also known as Plastic Crime wave, is a Chicago-based illustrator and writer, avant-garde musician, music historian and impresario… He writes and illustrates the 'Secret History of Chicago Music' comic in the *Chicago Reader* and cohosts WGN-AMs Secret History of Chicago Music Sites" (Rathode, 2018). Krakow emailed me questions to answer on behalf of my father to complete the article.

While cleaning out our family home prior to selling it, I came across clippings saved by my parents. One such clipping was an article written by Scott Yanow. "Since 1975, Scott Yanow had been a regular reviewer of albums in many jazz styles. He has written for many jazz and arts magazines including *JazzTimes*, *Jazziz*, *DownBeat*, *Cadence*, *Coda*, and the *Loss Angeles Jazz Scene* and was the jazz editor for *Record Review*" (Scott Yanow 2022).

My parents kept a clip from an article mentioning my dad, written by Scott Yanow in the *Cadence* magazine for April 1989. Another article found is from *Option*, discussing the *Honkers & Bar Walkers* volume 1 CD, and it was written by Scott Jackson.

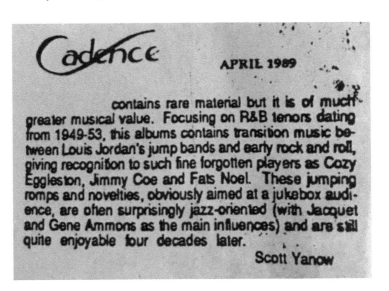

contains rare material but it is of much greater musical value. Focusing on R&B tenors dating from 1949-53, this albums contains transition music between Louis Jordan's jump bands and early rock and roll, giving recognition to such fine forgotten players as Cozy Eggleston, Jimmy Coe and Fats Noel. These jumping romps and novelties, obviously aimed at a jukebox audience, are often surprisingly jazz-oriented (with Jacquet and Gene Ammons as the main influences) and are still quite enjoyable four decades later.

Scott Yanow

OPTION

HONKERS & BAR WALKERS, VOL. 1 This collection documents the fallout in the early '50s from the rhythm & blues tenor sax explosion, originally set ablaze by the likes of Illinois Jacquet in the mid-'40s. Inspired by Jacquet, Lester Young and countless others, the lesser known talents assembled here play the real thing. Starting with the classic recording of "Night Train" by Jimmy Forrest, this rolls smoothly along to such delights as Cozy Eggleston's "Cozy's Beat," Jimmy Coe's "After Hours Joint," and Paul Bascomb's "Pink Cadillac" (not Bruce's). It's one long stroll through tenor madness. This is after-hours listening material, with a scotch and beer chaser at hand — smooth and soothing. If R&B honkers appeal to you, you can't go wrong with this collection of tenors, which manages to walk you through most of the stylistic tendencies of the period. (Delmark, 4243 N. Lincoln Ave., Chicago, IL 60618) — Scott Jackson

It's such an honor to know that people still want to write about my father. He received an honor right before his passing, from the renowned Refe Jazz Society. They've held their annual Hyde Park Jazz Festival since 2006. Musicians perform at the festival in Hyde Park, Kenwood, and the Washington Park areas of Chicago. My parents played in the festivals many times. The Jazz Society had to cancel its concerts during COVID-19. They are back on track to hold their next jazz festival on Saturday, September 24, 2022.

21

The Aftermath
The Current State of Jazz

Contemporary Jazz

Dad would always tell me, "Self-preservation is the first law of nature." Many of the jazz greats are no longer with us. However, new jazz artists today are preserving the art form. Jazz is not dead and continues to thrive. Today's jazz may not be the same as bebop, swing, and bool jazz, but it is aesthetically. In defining the aesthetics of music, it is "a branch of philosophy that deals with the nature of art, beauty and taste in music, and with the creation of appreciation of beauty in music" (https://en.m.wikipedia.org). Also, it has to do with the feelings and emotions we get while listening to music. In addition, the symbolic representation and sounds are parts of musical anesthetics. Music is an art "in one guise or another, permeates every human society. Modern music is heard in a bewildering profusion of styles, many of them contemporary, others engendered in past eras" (Epperson 2022).

What is the status and definition of the art form of jazz music today? Just like jazz from the past had different genres such as cool jazz or fusion, contemporary jazz does too. In describing old jazz, historians refer to it as traditional. The name given to describe the new jazz styles is contemporary: "Contemporary Jazz is an umbrella term for the diverse array of new music in the jazz idiom… The umbrella term encompasses two main subgenres: Modern jazz and smooth jazz" (MasterClass 2022).

Modern jazz

> Nowadays, the word "modern" is often used interchangeably with "contemporary" to describe a jazz sound. It's a rather vague term that covers a range of sub-genres, but generally refers to music that is more current than styles like saying, Bebop and modal jazz. (Discover Jazz 2022)

> The first and most obvious difference between modern and…over more traditional…is the sound…jazz forms sound more soft, soothing and generally module, modern jazz can be faster…harsher than traditional… Modern jazz, though often brilliant can be offbeat, difficult to follow, intrusive and possibly not the kind of thing you could have playing to say relax

your guest. Traditional jazz standards are often shorter than modern jazz compositions and contain lyrical content that most jazz compositions does not. (jstutler 2019)

To see and hear a video of a brief summary of jazz, go to https://youtu.be/bRaQgUIQLTQ.

To hear artist Ambrose Akinmusire play modern jazz, visit https://youtu.be//HIIfMI3Bkg.

It's complex to differentiate and understand music genres. The best explanation found is in the article "Best Modern Jazz Artists: Modern Jazz Explained in 2022" by Jayden Buckley, dated August 12, 2021.

Smooth jazz

There are several definitions and descriptions of smooth jazz. "By a vast majority, *smooth jazz is often regarded as 'contemporary' jazz or instrumental pop'.* To be more precise, urban jazz or contemporary jazz is to be regarded as a derivative of smooth jazz. It is a new style of music incorporating the key aspects of hip-hop." The article continues to define smooth jazz as "an extremely popular genre of music, the concept of 'smooth' jazz revolves around the same musical instruments associated with traditional jazz, and strongly reflects the influential elements of rock & roll, funk, rhythm &blues, and pop" (Roussey 2017).

The main difference between smooth jazz and traditional jazz is the pianist. With the pianist, there is no improvisation. Of the two types, smooth jazz is not about improvisation. However, improvisation is the main staple in modern jazz. The melody and rhythmic beats are the basis of smooth jazz instrumental music. Musicians use elastic guitars, synthesizers, lite-funk rhythms, trumpets, and alto or soprano saxophones. Some say, "Smooth jazz is an *outgrowth of fusion, one that emphasizes its polished side...* it relies on rhythms and grooves instead of improvisation" (Dean 2004)

Here are two good examples of smooth jazz sound. To hear them, visit https://youtu.be/K7RmhU4m2no and https://youtu.be/CdnaJPPxQow.

Current Generation of Jazz Artists

Jazz, stemming from its birthplace in New Orleans, has never been stagnant: "A younger generation of listeners have turned to... *Robert Glasper* and Kamasi Washington, who have helped jazz reclaim its relevance...keeping it alive" (Waring, 2021). Using improvisation and pairing their music with other types of music is their method of operating.

Kamasi Washington is an up-and-coming young jazz musician playing modern jazz. "One of the reasons that contemporary jazz is reconnecting with young people is down to the appeal of this LA-born saxophonist's transformative 2015 debut album *The Epic...* Like many of today's young jazz musicians, Washington's music is influenced as much by hip-hop jazz; he even appeared on *Kendrick Lamar's* visionary album *To Pimp a Butterfly.*" (Waring

2021). To hear Kamasi Washington, visit https://youtu.be/LTQQErG7Am8 (Montreal Jazz Festival 2022).

Christian Scott aTunde Adjuah is another current artist who plays modern jazz. He is a New Orleans-born "trumpeter with a clear, burnished tone who acknowledges the tradition of the music but sees the future of adult rock, African music, movie soundtracks, and hip hop. He describes his music as 'stretch music'…that refers to its elastic characteristics" (Waring 2021). To hear him play, visit https://youtu.be/LJDCpoKFDCo.

Many female jazz artists are on the horizon too. Nubya Garcia is one of them. She is a saxophonist from London. On her new album, *Source*, "the legacy of John Coltrane and Dexter Gordon came to mind…bless long notes… but it's more intense than the similarly described music of modern sax star Kamasi Washington" (Beeson 2020). To hear female artist Nubya Garcia, a tenor saxophonist, go to https://youtu.be/SJKmCz979Ek.

Another currently popular female jazz artist is Sheila Maurice-Grey from Britain, who plays the trumpet. She's played alongside other current female artists such as Nubya Garcia and Cassie Kinoshi. Early jazz artists who influenced her music style are Pharoah Sanders and John Coltrane. Current contemporary jazz artists who influence her are Moses Boyd and Shabaka Hutchings. To hear Sheila Maurice-Grey's music, visit https://youtu.be/SDKVQN9RLQ.

22

Conclusion

There are approximately seventy to one hundred stations playing jazz throughout the United States. Usually, while driving or at home, I listen to Sirius XM channel 46, the Heat, for their hot R and B and hip-hop. Also, I tune in to channel 48, Heart & Soul: Adult R&B Hits, and channel 49, Soul Town: Classic Soul & Motown. One day, while driving, switching radio stations, I happened upon a Sirius XM station called Watercolors playing jazz. "Watercolors is a *Sirius XM Radio* music channel that specializes in playing smooth jazz. It is available on channel 66 on Sirius XM Radio (where it replaced Jazz Café for that service on November 12, 2008), as well as channel 66 on *Dish Network*" (siriusxm.fandom.com).

Sirius XM has another channel that plays jazz. One can hear it on SiriusXM'S Real Jazz. Real Jazz is a Sirius XM satellite radio station. Sirius XM channel 67 was previously on channel 70. The channel plays traditional jazz, contemporary jazz, and bebop music. The Real Jazz channel 67 focuses on playing the classic sounds and styles of jazz artists. On channel 67, one can listen to jazz music played by past and current jazz artists. They feature music from Herbie Hancock, Wynton Marsalis, Marquis Hill, Jocelyn Gould, and Cannonball Adderley.

Actually, music heard on Real Jazz channel 67 sounds like the genre of jazz my parents played. People would ask my parents if they were blues jazz artists. Adamantly, they would say no. People would ask me the same thing. So I'd tell them the same thing. As mentioned earlier, saxophonist Lester Young influenced my father's style and his sound of play. Later, he did say he developed his own sound. From what I can remember, there was an improvisation in his band's music just like modern jazz. I don't want to pinpoint my parents having a specific style using today's categories. I know that because of their era of playing, it's more like traditional jazz. From today's perspective of categories, their sound resembles modern moreso than smooth jazz. On his album *Grand Slam*, my father says, "We are Chicago musicians playing Midwest funk." I wish I would have had more interest in my parents' music. I would've asked them more about their music and style. Now I can't. I can only give my assumptions and interpretations. One thing I know for sure: Music has no boundaries.

I've never been a connoisseur of jazz, but my preference in today's category in contemporary music is smooth jazz. It's so relaxing, peaceful, and serene. Despite my parents being jazz musicians, I've always listened to R and B, rap, and hip-hop music. In the group my siblings and I had, we only performed songs from that genre too. Since I came across the SiriusXM station's jazz on channel 66, that's the only music I prefer now. It took me all these years to listen to and appreciate jazz music.

I was going away to college at the University of Illinois Urbana-Champaign one fall. Before my freshman year that summer, my mother gave me my first lesson on her alto saxophone. She did tell me I had a good sound. I was so elated by her comments not because she was my mother. I felt pride in what she said about my sound because she was a renowned alto jazz saxophonist. People said she had a sound better than my dad's. I've been so moved while writing this book about my parents. I am thrilled about my newfound interest in jazz. It's inspired me so much that I've taken my mom's alto sax out of the closet.

I wanted her saxophone after my dad passed, and my siblings obliged. Upon my return home after Dad passed, I went to the music store. I purchased some reeds for the mouthpiece. I blew a few notes on the sax. I even searched for saxophone lessons. I haven't tried to play it since 2012—over ten years. Now I want to learn how to play my mom's saxophone. It's never too late. You may hear me on the radio, playing one day using my parent's Co-Egg record label. My dad helped me get my own label: Sweet C Records. After all, it is definitely in my genes. I'll carry the torch to continue my parents' legacy in music.

These are my dad's albums—*Grand Slam* (Stereo CE-3548) and *Whammin & Slammin* (Stereo B4RS-2393)—under Co-Egg Records and Eggton Publishing Company, produced by Cozy Eggleston, the cover and artwork done by Ralph Arnold. Cozy's love for baseball influenced the theme for his first album cover.

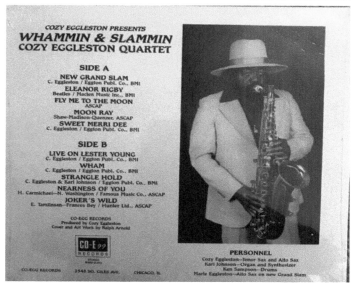

—MUSICAL AND DRAMATIC—
PRESENTING COZY EGGLESTON
and his combo. The Hi-O-Silver
man himself. Open late.
Mickey's Lounge, 5639 W. Roosevelt, Cicero, Ill.

● MULTI-REEDMAN Yusef
Lateef said it was just like his
old Chicago days back in 1948.
Lateef, who is playing around
the city this week, was referring to the all-out jam session
at the Living Room, 744 E.
83d st. where Merri Dee of
radio station WBEE was
having a benefit for cancer research Tuesday night.

When Lateef arrived at 3:15
a. m., after his own gig, the
session was still going strong.
Among the participants were
O. C. Smith, Red Holt, Prince
James, Odell Brown, Clarence
Wheeler and the Enforcers,
Tommy Jones, The Lloyd Wal-
lace Trio, Billy Mitchell, Ken
Chaney, and Cozy Eggleston.
[Ramsey Lewis was in the
audience, but couldn't play be-
cause of an injured finger.]
Lateef joined in, and the ses-
sion which began at 9 p. m.
went on till around 4:30 a. m.

Lateef, who plays tenor and
alto sax, flute, oboe, bassoon,
bamboo flutes, and other
assorted reeds, calls his music

Yusef Lateef

Lil Green Band Draw at Paradise

Lil Green, billed as queen of the blues, and her orchestra are much in evidence on the Paradise stage, with a program that is plenty hot.

Featured in the band are Howard Calendar and James Kendrichs, trumpeters, and Melvin Scott, Cozy Eggleston and Richard Fox, saxophonists. One number, "Concerto for Two Saxophones," develops into a battle royal between Scott and Fox.

Al Cowan's Musical Madcaps, seven males, offer songs and dances strictly in the groove.

Rae and Rae are fast dancers. Tim Moore and Vivian Harris provide comedy. To top it all Lil Green turns vocalist in topical tempo.

Articles from the Detroit Free Press on February 9, 1946. Cozy Eggleston and his Jazz Band performing at the Paradise Theatre in Detroit. The Theatre was in the Paradise Valley area in Detroit's Black business and entertainment center. The name of the Black residential area surrounding Paradise Valley was called Black Bottom. Google Cozy Eggleston for additional information about him and his music.

ORANGE COUNTY REGISTER

LP/CHROME cassette DL/DC-438

"Honkers & Bar Walkers" features eight lesser-known tenor players from the early '50s. The best-known is Jimmy Forrest whose celebrated recording of "Night Train" is included. The others (such as Cozy Eggleston, Jimmy Coe and Fred Jackson) are fine players. This is solid, unpretentious music which will appeal to anyone who enjoys the R&B/jazz sound.

Big Band Jazz: Tulsa to Harlem
LP/CHROME cassette DL/DC-439

Cab Calloway's band boasts a lineup of great players, but the emphasis, unfortunately, is on Cab's vocals. There are also two big-band jazz numbers directed by longtime Duke Ellington clarinetist Jimmy Hamilton. He plays tenor here, and these two cuts alone make the album worth owning.

— Jay Roebuck

CLEVELAND PLAIN DEALER
FRIDAY, MAY 5, 1989

By ROBERT DERWAE

Honkers & Bar Walkers (various artists) Delmark Records.

Illinois Jacquet, who today leads one of the best jazz orchestras around, almost singlehandedly established the "honking" style of tenor sax playing with his incendiary solo on Lionel Hampton's 1942 recording of "Flying Home." Before long, Jacquet's methods were *de rigueur* for saxmen working in the fledgling R&B style. Performance shtick designed to excite the crowd — leaping about the stage, playing while lying on the floor and waving feet in the air, and "walkin' " the length of the bar while honking and wailing — also became part and parcel of R&B.

Sound familiar? With the exception of tenor saxophonist Jimmy Forrest's slow-grind "Night Train," which was a giant hit in 1951 (and which is based on Duke Ellington's "Happy Go Lucky Local"), "Honkers and Bar Walkers" is a collection of lesser-known R&B tunes featuring sax leads in small group settings. Drawn from the vaults of two indie labels — the United/States combine and Regal — these early '50s tracks are good examples of the stylistic link in the jazz-to-R&B-to-rock evolution.

One of the better cuts, "Big Heavy (Blue Lites Boogie)," a medium-slow, finger-poppin' shuffle blues by Cozy Eggleston. was used by disc jockey Alan Freed during his tenure at WINS in New York. The recordings, most of which are slow to medium in tempo, speak directly and have a simple, undeniable appeal.

Derwae is a free-lance writer who covers jazz for The Plain Dealer.

Siouxland Happenings

"Morrie" Miller
Music Editor

FEB. 4-10, 1989

WHAT'S HAPPENING MAGAZINE

What a surprise, an outstanding collection of red hot sax sounds from a varied selection of prized tenor (and alto), saxophonists that is guaranteed to please any lover of authentic cool saxophone sounds.

Though possibly not as famous as legends Big Jay McNeely, Sam "The Man" Taylor, Sil Austin, Lee Allen, etc., never the less this collection provides an essential look at artists that for the most part became known largely due to the efforts of various independent record labels.

A vintage 1951 "Night Train" by St. Louis mainstay *Jimmy Forest* is a kicked back, ultra cool version of this popular song, from 1949 comes a most swinging track "Everybody Get Together," an open invitation to party, with this hot little jazz combo featuring *Ray Abrams* on tenor.

The blazing sax duo of *Cozy Eggleston* (tenor), and *Marie Eggleston* (alto), present three tracks from 1952, including a mighty "Big Heavy" (Blue Lites Boogie), along with a short but oh so sweet "Willow Weep For Me."

Look out, another party goin' down on "After Hours Joint" by (*Jimmy Cole* (tenor), describing jazz under ideal conditions, in the wee wee hours.

Additional gems include Lucius Tyson (a/k/a *Doc Sausage*) band featuring *Charlie Jackson* (tenor), on a red hot, "Sausage Rock", a familiar early 50's "Duck Fever" showcasing Fred Jackson on (tenor), four strong 1952 selections from *rats Noel* (tenor) including a beautifully rendered "Wish You Were Here", plus many more classic mouthwatering jazz offerings from other artists.

If you're practicing safe sax, better not get near this collection — this is the real deal. Pickup on the elements of jazz where cool is cool and hot is red hot!

COZY EGGLESTON'S ORGAN QUARTET & HIS REVUE

My cousin
Mrs. Mattie B. Rutledge
Cairo, Ill.

COZY EGGLESTON one of America's   Co-Egg Recording Artist
greatest tenor saxophone stars.

Grandma Mattie, Center
Cozy's Mother

References

Ash, J. 2018. "Getting Cozy in the Club." *AM, Then FM* (blog).

Ayer, J. 2005. As cited in Eastman School of Music, University of Rochester, Institute of Music Leadership, and Segregated Musician Union Locals. 2007

Beeson, A. 2020. "The New Cool: *Nubya Garcia Puts the Jazz Back in Modern Jazz.*" KNKX Public Radio.

Buckley, J. 2021. Play The Tunes, Music Genre, Next Modern Jazz Artists: *Modern Jazz. Explained in 2022*

Culture & Change: Black History in America (Scholastic Teacher's Activity Guide).

Dean, M. 2004. "The History of Smooth Jazz, What is Smooth Jazz?" A Collection of Opinions with History Impressions. AllMusic, www.smooth-jazz.de.

Discover Jazz. 2022. "What is Modern Jazz? *8 of the Best Contemporary Jazz Artists Today.*

Epperson, G. 2022. "Contemporary Jazz Guide: Origins of Contemporary Jazz." Master Class. https://www.masterclass.com/articles/contemporary-jazz-guide.

Fox, D. 2013. "In Honor of Tonight's Blue Moon, Here Are 10 Artists Performing the Classic Ballad." https://965kvki.com/in-honor-of-the-blue-moon-here-are-10-artists-performing-the-classic-ballad/.

Fripp, M. 2021. "10 Best Hard Bop Albums." Jazzfuel.

Gerds, E. 1969. "Night Beat—Jazz is the Thing They Do Best."

Grossman, R. "Before Uber there was Jitney." *Chicago Tribune*, March 9, 2014.

History.com editors. 2009. "Harlem Renaissance." History. Updated January 12, 2022.

https://www.dictionary.com

https://pophistorydig.com/topics/tag/billie-holiday-artie shaw.

https://siriusxm.fandom.com

https://www.thejazzpianosite.com

Jackson, S. "Option." Honkers & Bar Walkers, vol.1, n.d.

jazzstandards.com/history/index.htm.

Jet (magazine). 1955. Vol. 8, no. 15. Johnson Publication Company.

Jones, A. 2019. "This Is the True History of Double Dutch." PushBlack Now. https://www.pushblack.us/news/ true-history-double-dutch.

Jones, J. 2018. Flashbak, Everything Old Is New Again. flashbak.com.

Kieffer, M. 1985. "Hidden Treasures, Honoring Scores of Little known People and Places that Celebrate Chicago's Earthly Spirit." Chicago.

Martinez, R., and B. Krefft. 2022. "Regal Theater." Cinema Treasures. cinematreasures.org

merriam-webster.com. s.v. "ragtime" https://www.merri- amwebster.com/dictionary/ragtime.

Pruter, R. D. 2014. "the Moonglows." *Britannica*.

PianoTV. 2018. "A Simple Guide to American Music History."

Roussey, B. 2017. "Can Smooth and Contemporary Jazz Be Considered Music?" Merriam School of Music, Brass & Woodwinds Archives. www.merriammusic. com.

RST Record. 1994. Chicago Jump Bands, Early R & B, Vol.1, 1945–1943.

Strathdee, Russ, and Gary Copeland. 2010. "Russ's Old 78s—R&B Album." Russ and Gary's "The Best Years of Music." strathdee.wordpress.com.

Saith, S. "Sunset in Bronzeville: In a Place of Jazz Legends, Al Capone, Machine Politics and a Family Legacy, Meyers Ace Hardware Soon to Be History." *Seth Saith* (blog), January 26, 2017.

Stutler, J. "Jazz Now and Jazz Then: What's the Difference?" *The RazMaJazz Dixie Jazz Band* (blog), April 27, 2019.

Wallenfeldt, J. 2020. "the Green Book." *Britannica.*

Waring, C. 2021. "17 Modern Jazz Musicians Shaping the Future of Jazz." udiscovermusic.com.

Wharton Center. 2015. "The Varying Styles of Jazz: A Road Map." *Lansing State Journal.*

Wikipedia.

About the Author

Connie J. Eggleston MSW, CPM currently resides in Oklahoma City, Oklahoma. However, she was born and reared in Chicago, Illinois. It's a city well known for its jazz. She grew up around jazz. Both parents played the saxophone. Her father formed his own band, of which her mother was a member. They performed throughout the United States. Her parents were prominent jazz artists with an interesting history. This inspired her to write a book about them. She wanted to capture the story of their lives in writing. A book was one way to leave a written legacy for her parents. She started recording her dad telling his story after her mom passed. Thus came her first novel, *The Life and Times of Cozy Eggleston and His Jazz Band: Featuring His Wife, Marie Stone*.

Connie developed an interest in writing in high school. She enjoyed reading books and writing reports for class assignments. She honed her writing skills as an English major in college. Later in life, during her twenty-six-year career in state government, she became a grant writer, successfully obtaining operating funds for the organization. Connie wrote white papers, program evaluation reports, and research papers. In addition, the *Southwestern Journal of Aging* featured an article she wrote in its publication. Writing this book gave her the impetus to write another one, so be on the lookout.

CPSIA information can be obtained
at www.ICGtesting.com
Printed in the USA
LVHW070056010723
751015LV00012B/84